THE KINGFISHER

First

Animal
Encyclopedia

NEW YORK

Editor Camilla Reid
Designers Steven Laurie, Ana Baillarguet

U.S. Editor Aimee Johnson
Proofreader Nikky Twyman

Photography Lyndon Parker, Andy Teare
Prop Organizer Michelle Callan
DTP Operator Primrose Burton

Artwork Archivist Wendy Allison
Assistant Artwork Archivist Steve Robinson
Picture Research Nic Dean

Production Controller Richard Waterhouse
U.S. Production Manager Oonagh Phelan

Cover Design Reg Page

Writers John Farndon, Jon Kirkwood

Consultant Toby Stark
Specialist Consultant Andrew Kemp
General Consultant Tom Schiele

**Produced for Kingfisher
by Warrender Grant Publications Ltd.**

KINGFISHER
a Houghton Mifflin Company imprint
215 Park Avenue South
New York, New York 10003
www.houghtonmifflinbooks.com

First published in 1998
6 8 10 9 7 5

5TR/0602/TWP/PW/150ENSOMA

LIBRARY OF CONGRESS CATALOGING-IN-PUBLICATION DATA
Kirkwood, Jon.
The Kingfisher first animal encyclopedia / Jon Kirkwood, John
Farndon. — 1st ed.
p. cm.
Summary: Text and illustrations present information on a variety
of animals from aardvarks and butterflies to whales and zebras.
1. Animals—Encyclopedias, Juvenile. [1. Animals—
Encyclopedias.] I. Farndon, John. II. Title.
QL49.K57 1998
590'.3—dc21   97-51609 CIP AC

ISBN: 0-7534-5135-2
Printed in Singapore

Your book

Your *First Animal Encyclopedia* is the perfect way of finding out all about the exciting world of animals. Packed with fascinating information, interesting activities, and brilliant pictures, it can be used for school projects or just for fun.

◁ The information about each picture is printed next to it. The arrows show you which information goes with which picture.

◁ Some pictures follow a sequence. Look out for the numbers to make sure you follow them in the right order.

▽ Step-by-step instructions show you how to do the activities.

1

2

Fact box
• These boxes contain extra information, facts, and figures.

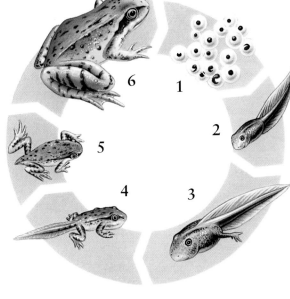

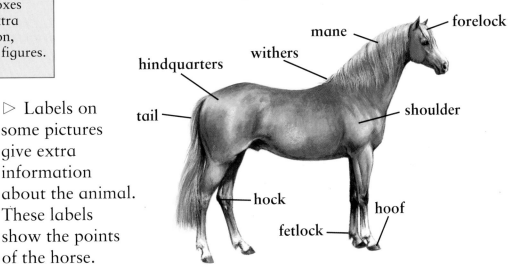

mane

forelock

withers

hindquarters

tail

shoulder

hock

hoof

fetlock

▷ Labels on some pictures give extra information about the animal. These labels show the points of the horse.

Find out more

If you want to find out more about each topic, look at this box. It will tell you which pages to look at.

Contents

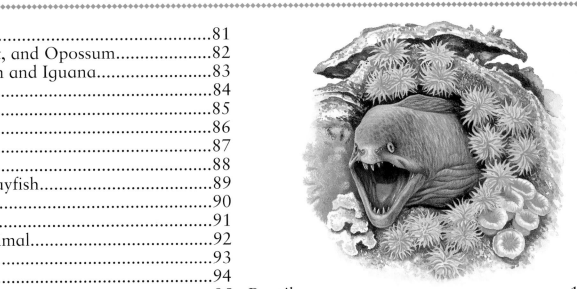

Aardvark

The aardvark is an African mammal that eats termites and ants. Its hearing is so sharp that it can detect these insects moving underground.

◁ The aardvark tears away at termite nests to get at the juicy insects inside. Once the galleries and chambers of the nest are opened up, it quickly licks up the termites.

◁ The word aardvark means "earth pig" in the Afrikaans language. This name was given to them by Dutch settlers in Africa. Aardvarks are the same size as pigs, but they have much larger ears and longer snouts.

◁ Inside the aardvark's huge snout there is a 12-inch-long sticky tongue. It is well designed for probing into insect mounds.

◁ Aardvarks live in burrows under the ground. If threatened by a lion, they use their strong claws to dig themselves a deep hole to hide in.

Find out more
Ant and Termite
Anteater

Albatross

Albatrosses are the biggest of all seabirds. They live in the cold Southern Hemisphere, where they survive on fish and seawater. Albatrosses can glide for great distances on their huge wings, and are able to fly 10,000 miles in a single trip over the ocean.

△ The albatross has the longest wings of any bird—nearly 13 feet from tip to tip. It often flies without flapping its wings at all. Instead, it skims close to the waves and uses the wind to help it along.

▽ Albatrosses only return to land to raise their young. When the young birds are ten months old, they leave the island where they were born and stay at sea for several years.

Fact box

• Albatross eggs take 80 days to hatch—longer than any other species of bird.
• To feed, albatrosses settle on the ocean and catch squid.
• An albatross can travel as far as 500 miles in just 12 hours.

Find out more
Bird
Gull
Penguin
Puffin
Seabird

Alligator and Crocodile

Alligators and crocodiles are large reptiles that live in rivers and swamps in tropical areas. They float beneath the surface of the water, with only their eyes and nostrils showing, ready to snap up fish, turtles, and even big mammals in their huge jaws.

△ Crocodiles are cold-blooded creatures. They spend some of their time in the water, keeping cool and hunting. Crocodiles also spend time sunbathing on the riverbank, where they can absorb enough heat to keep active.

◁▽ The American alligator (left) has a broader and shorter jaw than the crocodile (below). Both alligators and crocodiles have between 60 and 80 teeth in their powerful jaws. They use the teeth to rip their prey to pieces.

Fact box

• Crocodiles have existed for over 200 million years.
• Alligators can grow up to 20 feet long.
• The largest, the saltwater crocodile, grows to almost 27 feet.

▽ Alligators and crocodiles lay up to 90 eggs in a nest on the riverbank made from mud and leaves. When the young hatch, they call to their mother, she digs them out, picks them up gently in her mouth, and carries them down to the water.

Find out more
Komodo dragon
and Iguana
Lizard

Amphibian

Amphibians are animals that live both in the water and on the land. Frogs, toads, newts, and caecilians are all amphibians. They are found everywhere except Antarctica, particularly in warm places.

△ Newts have long tails and four short legs, and they look like lizards. However, they do not have scales and their skin is moist.

△ Adult frogs and toads have four legs and no tail. Some frogs inflate their throats to make a loud croak. This helps them attract a mate.

▷ Caecilians have no legs and are similar to worms. They live underground in tropical places. Unlike most amphibians, the female caecilian guards her eggs.

◁ 1 A homemade minipond is a great way of attracting frogs and newts to your backyard. You will need a plastic bowl, some sand, pondweed, and a few stones and rocks.

◁ 2 Dig a hole in a corner of your yard and drop the bowl into it. Cover the bottom with the sand and stones, making sure that some of the rocks rise above the surface of the water. Add the pondweed, then fill the bowl with water. Over the next few weeks, watch to see if your pond has any visitors.

Find out more
Fish
Frog and Toad
Lizard
Newt
Reproduction

Anaconda

The anaconda is one of the largest snakes in the world. It can weigh up to 220 pounds, which is as much as a large pig. It lives in the jungles of South America, where it hunts in the trees and rivers for food.

▽ The anaconda is called a "constrictor" because it constricts, or squeezes, its prey to death, instead of poisoning it. Anacondas can attack prey as large as a coypu, an animal like a beaver that lives in and near water. The snake will not need to eat for a month after it has eaten a coypu.

△ This anaconda is fairly small. The biggest ones are as thick as your waist and over 15 feet long—about as big as a car.

◁ Snake skin will not stretch like human skin, so the anaconda has to shed its skin as it grows. The old skin splits when it gets too tight, and the snake rubs it off against a branch. Underneath the old skin, there is a shiny new one.

Find out more
Cobra
Rattlesnake

Ant and Termite

Ants and termites live in enormous nests called colonies. Inside most nests there is a queen who lays eggs, and thousands of workers who run the colony and feed her. Each worker has a job to do—some act as soldiers, guarding the nest, others gather food, and cleaners keep it tidy.

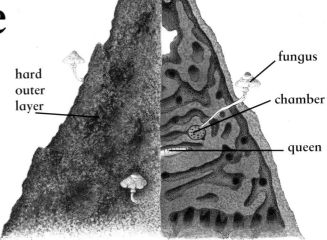

hard outer layer

fungus

chamber

queen

△ In grassland areas, termites build castles of mud that are 23 feet tall. Most termites feed on plants, but some live off a fungus that grows in their nests.

▽ A fungus grows in the nests of leafcutter ants. The ants take bits of leaf to the fungus, which "eats" the leaf and gives off sugars for the ants to eat.

king

queen

worker

soldier

◁ The queen of a termite nest lays 30,000 eggs a day. She can be 4 inches long. The king can grow to almost an inch, and the soldiers and workers are about half as big.

▷ Army ants march in vast swarms that can be 40 feet wide. They prey on insects and small animals. The worker ants take the prey back to the nest while the soldier ants stand guard. Termites are sometimes called white ants, but termites have softer bodies and wider waists than ants.

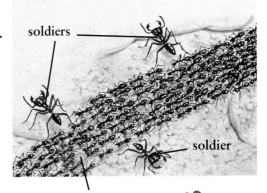

soldiers

soldier

workers

◁ Although not as tall as a termite's nest, there are lots of compartments inside an ant's nest. This is where eggs are laid and where young ants are cared for. Food is stored here, too.

Find out more
Aardvark
Anteater
Bee and Wasp
Insect

Anteater

Anteaters are mammals from South and Central America. Besides eating ants, they feed on termites and other bugs. They may look strange, but their pointy snout, sticky tongue, and sharp claws make them perfectly designed for the job of breaking into insect mounds and licking up the tasty creatures inside.

△ The collared anteater catches the termite at home in its nest, high in the trees. Using its long tail to balance itself, the anteater will suck up thousands of termites in just a few minutes.

▷ Giant anteaters shuffle along slowly, carrying their weight on the knuckles of their forefeet to keep their claws sharp for digging. In its first year, a young anteater hitches a ride on its mother's back.

◁ The collared anteater lives in trees in the rain forest. It has a prehensile (gripping) tail. It is one of only two anteaters that live off the ground. They are active at night, sleeping mainly during the day.

Find out more
Aardvark
Ant and Termite
Mammal
Porcupine
Sloth

Antelope

Antelope graze on the wide plains of Africa and Asia and can run fast. There are many different types of antelope. They range in size from the royal antelope, which is 10 inches tall at the shoulder, to the giant eland, which is almost 6 feet tall. Male antelope, and sometimes females, have curved horns.

▽ The addax is a rare antelope that lives in the Sahara. Its horns are long and twisted. The hooves are broad to help it walk on soft sand.

◁ Wildebeest, or gnu, are antelope that migrate in huge herds of up to 500,000. They follow the rain to find rich pastures. Wildebeest are the most common wild grazing animals in East Africa.

▷ Oryx have long, sharp horns and black-and-white faces. They live in the deserts of Arabia and Africa. Two oryx species, the Arabian and the scimitar oryx, have been hunted until there are very few left in the world.

◁ Springboks are small, graceful antelope that live on the open plains of southern Africa. These animals, which have bold markings, can be 30 inches tall. Their name comes from the way they leap, or spring, into the air.

Find out more

Camel
Deer
Llama
Reindeer
Zebra

13

Arctic tern

Arctic terns make the longest of all animal journeys. In the fall, after nesting on the Arctic coastline, these small seabirds fly south to spend a few months fishing on the other side of the world, in the Antarctic Ocean. In the spring, they make the long trip north again to breed.

◁ Arctic terns lay two or three eggs in nests on the frozen Arctic ground, or tundra. They defend their eggs and chicks by diving at attacking predators.

△ The Arctic tern's round trip may be more than 22,000 miles. But, by being at each pole in the summertime, it spends nearly all its life in daylight. Chicks hatch in the northern summer, and by fall they are ready to make the marathon flight south with their parents.

▽ Sooty and fairy terns are found on tropical islands. Unlike Arctic terns, they do not migrate.

sooty tern

fairy tern

Find out more
Albatross
Gull
Migration
Seabird

Armadillo

Armadillos are armor-plated mammals related to anteaters and sloths. They are found in regions of North America and all through South America. There are 20 species —the largest is the giant armadillo, which is 5 feet long.

△ Armadillos live alone, in pairs, or in small groups in burrows. They come out at night to feed. They are easily frightened and bolt for their burrows when threatened.

◁ Armadillos eat many different kinds of plants, insects, and small animals. They like ants and termites, which they dig up with their powerful front legs and claws.

▽ When in danger, armadillos roll up into a ball, showing only the hard plates on their head and tail.

Fact box

• Despite their heavy armor, armadillos swim well. To help them float, they swallow air.
• The smallest armadillo is the pink fairy armadillo, which is 6 inches long.
• The most common is the nine-banded armadillo.

Find out more
Aardvark
Ant and Termite
Anteater
Hedgehog
Sloth

Baboon

Baboons are large monkeys that live in troops of over 100 in number. They feed on many different foods, from seeds, fruit, and grasses to small animals and eggs. They are found in Arabia and in Africa, south of the Sahara.

△ Baboons spend much of their time grooming each other. This helps form bonds between babies and mothers, and also between members of the troop. The troop is usually made up of related females, males, and one lead male.

▽ Mandrills, from the West African rain forests, are cousins of the baboon. They have bare patches on their large faces. In adult males, these are brightly colored.

▷ The gelada is a monkey similar to a baboon found in the mountains of Ethiopia, in East Africa. It has a hairless red patch in the center of its chest, from which it gets its other name —the "bleeding heart baboon." The males have very long hair over their head and shoulders.

Fact box
• Baboons sometimes weigh 88 pounds. They can be nearly 4 feet long, and have tails of 27 inches.
• Male baboons are twice as big as females.
• Baboons bark like dogs when frightened.

Find out more
Chimpanzee
Gorilla
Monkey
Orangutan

Baby animal

When they are young, many animals need care, just as human babies do. Their parents must keep them safe from harm and find food for them until they are old enough to take care of themselves.

△ When danger threatens, the male mouthbreeder fish shelters his young in his mouth. He spits them out as soon as it is safe.

△ The merganser duck sometimes gives its babies a piggyback ride. This keeps them safe until they are old enough to swim by themselves.

△ A zebra foal must learn to walk right after it is born so it can follow its mother away from danger. The male zebras will protect the herd by kicking and biting any attackers.

△ Emperor penguins keep their babies warm by carrying them on their feet.

◁ Play the baby penguin game with four or more people. Divide into two teams and stand in rows. The aim is to pass a beanbag along each row using only your feet. The first team to get the beanbag along the row wins.

Find out more

Alligator and Crocodile

Gorilla

Mammal

Penguin

Reptile

Badger

Badgers are powerful creatures, but they are also shy. They are related to skunks and, like them, have black-and-white markings. In Europe, they live in family groups in woodlands.

▽ Badgers are omnivores, which means that they eat all kinds of food. Their diet includes grasses, fruit, and nuts, as well as small animals and eggs. They are good at digging and often catch earthworms.

▽ Badgers are most active in the evening. This is when they come out to feed and to collect straw for bedding.

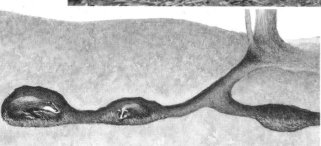

◁ During the day, badgers stay in underground burrows. As the group of badgers grows bigger, they dig more chambers. Some large burrows have been used for hundreds of years.

▷ Unlike the European badger, the American badger lives alone for most of the year in dry, open countryside. It also has a different face pattern.

Find out more
Mole
Skunk
Weasel

18

Bat

Bats have big ears, furry bodies, and wings like leather. They are nocturnal mammals. This means they sleep in caves and attics during the day and fly out to feed at night.

▽ Bats are the only mammals that can fly. They are very fast and acrobatic. When they chase insects, they twist and turn in midair.

△ Bats use sound to catch insects in the darkness. They send out high-pitched squeals that humans cannot hear. The echoes that bounce back tell the bats exactly where they will find their prey.

Fact box
• The "bumblebee," or hog-nosed bat may be the world's smallest mammal. It is less than an inch long.
• The South American vampire bat feeds on the blood of living animals.

▷ Flying foxes, or fruit bats, are large bats that live in tropical Africa and Asia. They eat mostly fruit. Flying foxes are important because they help spread the pollen and seeds of many plants.

Find out more
Bird
Insect
Mouse

Bear

The bear is the largest meat-eating animal on Earth. There are many kinds of bears, and most of them live in northern parts of the world. Their thick fur coats protect them from the cold.

kodiak bear

brown bear

polar bear

black bear

△ Most bears are large and powerful, with strong claws and a good sense of smell. The Kodiak bear of Alaska is the largest of all. It weighs almost 1,800 pounds and, when standing up, can be 13 feet tall.

◁ In winter, some bears find a snug place to hibernate. Hibernation is a very deep sleep that may last many weeks. The workings of the bear's body slow down to save energy.

◁ In the fall, American black bears hunt salmon and eat berries and honey. This helps them put on the weight they need in order to survive their long hibernation.

Find out more
Mammal
Polar bear
Raccoon

Beaver

Beavers live near rivers in North America and northern Europe. They are great builders and use their massive front teeth to cut down trees. Beavers use these trees to make their homes, which are called lodges.

Fact box

• Beaver dams can be over 1,600 feet long and up to 13 feet high.
• Some beaver dams are 1,000 years old.
• A male and female pair of beavers will stay together for their whole lives.

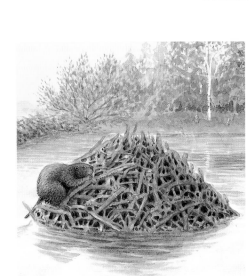

△ Beavers dam the river with branches to make a pond. In this pond they will build their lodge. Beavers use their webbed feet and big, flat tails to push themselves through the water. If alarmed, they slap their tails on the water to warn other beavers.

◁ Beaver lodges are made of sticks and mud. Beavers seal their lodges with more mud during the winter. The mud freezes hard and helps keep out predators.

▽ The adults enter the lodge by an underwater entrance and bring food to their young hidden inside. The young beavers will stay with their family for about two years. Then they leave to build their own lodges.

dam

lodge

Find out more

Mouse
Otter
Rabbit and Hare
Rat

Bee and Wasp

Bees and wasps are easy insects to spot because of their black-and-yellow, or black-and-white, striped bodies. Wasps and worker bees have a stinging tail. Bees only sting in self-defense and usually die afterward.

▽ Honeybees are ruled by a queen. They build wax rooms, called cells. **1** The queen lays an egg in each cell. **2** This grows into a larva. **3, 4** The worker bees feed it. **5, 6** Soon it grows into an adult and emerges.

△ Bees collect the sweet juice, or nectar, from flowers and use it to make honey. They keep the honey in cells to feed their growing young.

◁ The bumblebee is larger and more furry than the honeybee. It collects pollen from flowers using its hind legs. Flowers need bees to spread pollen from one flower to another. This way, the flowers can reproduce.

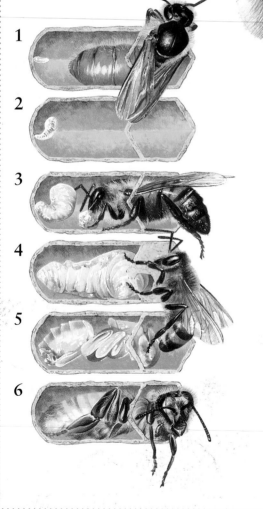

1

2

3

4

5

6

▽ Wasps are different from bees because they feed their young on insects, not honey. They use their sting to kill the insects. Adult wasps eat the sugars found in fruit, and so are attracted by the smell of sweet food or liquids.

Find out more

Ant and Termite

Fly

Insect

Beetle

There are over a quarter of a million species of beetle in the world. They come in many shapes and sizes, but all have one thing in common—a pair of delicate, folded wings protected by a hard outer casing, or shell.

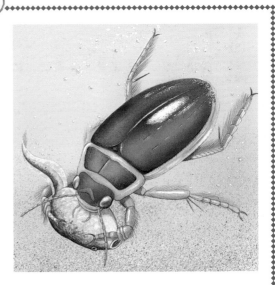

△ Some species of water beetle hunt tadpoles and baby fish. Before diving, the beetles come to the surface to collect air under their wing casings.

◁ Fireflies are not flies, but flying beetles that glow in the dark. They give off light from their abdomen (rear body part) to attract mates. They let out short, regular flashes—each species has its own typical flash pattern. In some of the 1,900 species the female does not fly. She is called a glowworm.

△ Dung beetles collect a ball of dung and lay an egg in it. When the egg hatches, the new beetle larva eats the dung.

▽ Stag beetles are huge, measuring up to 3 inches long. The males often fight each other with their large jaws.

Find out more

Ant and Termite
Dragonfly and Damselfly
Fly
Insect

Bird

Birds live all over the world, and there are nearly 10,000 species. They are the only animals to have feathers and wings, but not all can fly. All birds lay eggs, and most build nests where they can raise their chicks.

◁ Most birds, like this magpie, have a very light skeleton, strong chest muscles, a tough beak, and eyes on the side of the head. Nearly all birds make sounds, called songs, to "talk" to each other.

▷ Birds have evolved to fit the places where they live and the foods they eat. Birds of prey, like this sparrow-hawk, have strong claws, sharp eyes, and hooked beaks to help catch tiny animals hidden in the grass far below them.

▽ Birds often have dull feathers to help them hide among their surroundings. But some, like these male birds of paradise, are brightly colored. This helps them attract females.

blue bird of paradise

raggiana bird of paradise

black-billed touraco

rose-ringed parakeet

△ Many birds live on or near water. The jaçana has large feet and long claws, which help it to walk on floating leaves. Unlike most birds, it is the male jaçana that looks after the eggs, not the female.

Find out more
Eagle
Evolution
Ostrich, Emu, and Cassowary
Parrot
Penguin

Bison and Musk ox

The American bison, which is also called the plains buffalo, is the largest animal in North America. Despite their size, bison are agile and can run very fast. They are grazers, which means they feed on plants and grass.

▽ Bison live in small groups. Males and females live apart except in the mating season, when males will fight for females. At one time there were nearly 50 million bison in North America, but settlers hunted them so they nearly became extinct.

Fact box
• European bison are taller than the American bison, but not as heavy.
• Hunters killed all but about 1,000 of the American bison.
• Bison now survive in managed herds.

◁ Musk oxen are grazers like bison, but they live in the Arctic. Here their thick coats protect them from the winter cold.

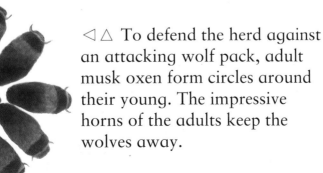

◁ △ To defend the herd against an attacking wolf pack, adult musk oxen form circles around their young. The impressive horns of the adults keep the wolves away.

Find out more
Antelope
Buffalo
Cow and Bull
Mammal
Yak

Buffalo

Buffalo are big, strong, dark-colored mammals with huge horns. African buffalo live in herds of several hundred—usually near water, since they love to wallow in mud. Water buffalo are found in the wetter areas of Asia. Few are found in the wild now, and they are mostly kept as farm animals.

△ African buffalo have a very bad temper, so humans have never managed to tame them.

Fact box
- When looking for insects, egrets (right) use buffalo as perches.
- The horns of the water buffalo are the biggest in the animal kingdom.
- Like cows, buffalo chew their cud, bringing once-eaten food back up for a second chew.

△ Males are much larger than females. Their horns meet together as a lump on their heads. This helps protect them from any attack. Groups of lions attack females and young, but they will rarely go for a male.

◁ Water buffalo have been domesticated for 3,000 years. They are used to pull carts and plows, but they can be kept for their meat, milk, and hides. Only a few survive in the wild in Asia, but buffalo released in Australia now run free in the swamps of the Northern Territory.

Find out more
Bison and
Musk ox
Cow and Bull
Mammal

Butterfly and Moth

These flying insects are found worldwide, especially in warm places. Most butterflies are colorful and fly by day. Moths fly at night and are usually dull in coloring.

△ Swallowtail butterflies have tails on their wings that look like the tails of swallows.

1 egg

2 caterpillar

3 pupa

4 adult

△ **1** The female butterfly lays her eggs on a branch, and these hatch into caterpillars. **2, 3** The caterpillar eats the leaves and grows fast, until it is ready to spin itself a hard case, called a pupa. **4** Over time, it starts to change and soon becomes an adult butterfly.

▽ The death's head hawk moth of Africa gets its name from the skull-shaped pattern on its back.

◁ See for yourself how caterpillars turn into butterflies. Collect some caterpillars and put them in a large jar, along with the branches you found them on. Attach some mesh across the top with a rubber band. Add fresh leaves every day and watch the changes as they happen. Make sure you let the butterflies go as soon as they can fly.

Find out more
Bee and Wasp
Cricket and Grasshopper
Insect
Reproduction

Camel

Camels live in the world's driest deserts. They have humps of fat on their backs that help them survive for days without food or water.

▽ A camel's feet are big and wide to stop it from sinking into the desert sand.

△ Camels have been used since ancient times to carry people across deserts.

△ A camel has two rows of eyelashes to shield its eyes in a sandstorm. It can also close its nostrils tight.

◁ The Arabian camel, or dromedary, has one hump. The Bactrian camel has two humps. Bactrians live in Central Asia; dromedaries live in North Africa, the Middle East, and India.

Find out more
Antelope
Cow and Bull
Giraffe
Llama

Camouflage

Many animals use camouflage—body shapes, colors, or markings that make them blend in with their background. Camouflage helps animals hide when hunting or being hunted.

△ The tiger's stripes help it blend in with the tall grass on the sunny, open plains where it lives. This makes the tiger hard to spot as it waits to ambush its prey.

◁ The flounder hides by lying flat on the ocean floor and changing color to match the sand and pebbles.

△ **1** Play a camouflage game with some friends. First you need to find three or four everyday objects, such as a can, a bottle, and a carton. Then stick leaves, grass, and scraps of paper to them. Finally, paint them with brown or green paint.

▷ Leaf insects look almost the same as a leaf. They also move slowly to try to fool predators into thinking they are leaves. Even their eggs are leaf-shaped.

▷ **2** Take the objects into the backyard and put them among the plants. Tell your friends what you have hidden and challenge them to find the objects. The person who finds the most things wins.

Find out more
Chameleon
Evolution
Tiger
Zebra

Cat (domestic)

All the domestic or house cats of today are descended from wildcats. They were first tamed over 4,000 years ago in ancient Egypt. Although domestic cats are fed by humans, they are still hunters like their ancestors, and have the same sharp teeth, pointed claws, and sensitive eyes for seeing in the dark.

tortoiseshell

blue tabby

chocolate point Siamese

▷ There are now over 40 different breeds of cat. Some, like the Siamese, have short hair. Others, like Persian cats, are long haired.

◁ Cats make good pets because they are clean, quiet, and friendly. They can be very independent, but they still need to be well cared for. Kittens have to be trained so they get used to humans and develop good habits in the home. They enjoy human contact, especially being stroked.

▷ The African wildcat is probably the domestic cat's main ancestor, although other cats have also been taken from the wild and tamed by humans. African wildcats look like domestic tabbies, but they are slightly bigger. Their fur is also thicker and the markings are not as bold.

African wildcat   domestic cat

Find out more
Cat (wild)
Cheetah
Leopard
Lion
Mammal
Puma

Cat (wild)

Except for the big cats like lions and tigers, most wild members of the cat family are fairly small. Many wild cats are hunted for their boldly patterned coats. Because of this, some are in real danger of extinction and need protection in the wild.

▷ Caracals are cats that live in dry, scrubby areas of India and Africa. They particularly like to eat birds and will often leap up to catch them. The saying "Putting the cat among the pigeons" comes from the actions of this cat.

△ The European wildcat is found in forests from western Asia, through the continent of Europe, to Scotland. They are nocturnal animals that hunt birds and small mammals for food. The female gives birth to between three and six kittens.

Fact box

• The smallest cat is the rusty-spotted cat, at just 14 inches long. It lives in India.
• The fishing cat of India has webbed paws.
• European wildcats can be 16 inches tall at the shoulder and weigh up to 22 pounds.

△ The North American bobcat gets its name from its short (bobbed) tail. It lives in forests and deserts and catches rabbits, mice, and squirrels.

Find out more

Cat (domestic)
Leopard
Lion
Tiger

Centipede

Many animals are so small that they can only be seen under a magnifying glass. We call these animals minibeasts. Minibeasts are invertebrates, which means that they have no backbone.

millipede

centipede

△ The hard bodies of centipedes and millipedes are split into segments. While centipedes have one pair of legs per segment, millipedes have two. Centipedes eat other invertebrates; millipedes are plant-eaters.

◁ There are many types of minibeast. Spiders are arachnids, and they have eight legs.

▷ Wood lice are land-living crustaceans, a group normally found in water.

◁ Yellow jackets are insects. They have six legs, and bodies with three sections.

wood

stone

plastic container

leaves and food scraps

▷ Snails are mollusks that carry their shells on their backs.

△ A good way of catching minibeasts is by making a trap. Put a plastic container in a hole and add some leaves, twigs, and scraps of food. Cover it with a piece of wood supported on stones. Leave your trap overnight. How many types of minibeast did you catch?

Find out more
Bee and Wasp
Insect
Slug and Snail
Spider
Worm

◁ Worms belong to a group called the annelids. They have long, soft bodies that are divided into many segments.

Chameleon

Chameleons are unusual lizards that can change their skin color. They do this when they are angry or frightened, when the light or temperature levels change, or to hide themselves.

△ There are special cells called melanophores underneath a chameleon's skin. These can change color to match the chameleon's surroundings, making it more difficult to see.

▽ A chameleon will sit in a tree waiting to catch insects. A strong, curled tail holds it to the branch, while swiveling eyes allow it to look forward and backward at the same time. Then its long tongue darts out to catch its prey.

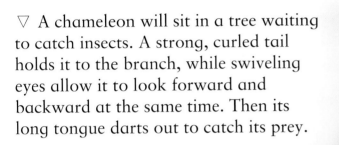

Fact box

• There are about 100 species of chameleon.
• Around 50 of these species live on the island of Madagascar.
• Chameleons usually live in trees, but come down to lay their eggs in the soil.

▷ The Madagascan pygmy chameleon is the smallest species at about an inch long. It lives mainly on leaves on the forest floor. Most chameleons are between 7 and 10 inches long, but some can grow up to 24 inches. Most chameleons eat insects, and the bigger ones also eat birds.

Find out more
Alligator and Crocodile
Cobra
Lizard
Reptile

Cheetah

Cheetahs are slim, spotted cats with long legs. They are the fastest land animals and can reach speeds of over 60 miles per hour. Cheetahs are found in the open plains of Africa, south of the Sahara.

△ Cheetahs can only run at high speed for a short distance They bring down their prey by tripping them.

◁ Female cheetahs have up to four babies at a time. The cubs have a long coat of gray hair, which makes them look like honey badgers. Honey badgers are aggressive animals, so other animals will not go near them. This "disguise" keeps the cubs safe from harm.

Fact box
• Cheetahs are the only cats that cannot draw their claws back fully. They use them to grip while sprinting after prey.
• Cheetahs are 4.5 feet long and have tails measuring 30 inches.

▷ Cheetahs once lived in North Africa, the Middle East, and India. But they have been trapped and tamed in Asia, and are now seriously endangered. Cheetahs are also rare in Africa.

Find out more
Cat (wild)
Leopard
Lion
Puma
Tiger

Chicken and Turkey

Chickens and turkeys are kept as farm animals all over the world. They are related to wild birds that were tamed by humans over 4,000 years ago. Chickens and turkeys can fly for short distances, but they prefer to walk or run.

△ Barnyard chickens eat seeds and small insects. They will also peck grain that is sprinkled on the ground. On some big farms, however, hens are fed special food and kept in small cages.

△ Male chickens are called roosters and have large crests on their heads and a ruff of long feathers around their necks. They often make a loud crow, especially at daybreak. Female chickens are called hens. They are smaller and less colorful than roosters. Hens are kept for both their meat and their eggs.

◁ Turkeys are big birds with a fleshy red "wattle" around their necks. They come from North and Central America, and were brought to Europe in about 1519 by Spanish explorers.

Find out more
Bird
Duck and Goose
Peacock
Pigeon and Dove
Swan

Chimpanzee

Chimpanzees, or chimps, are our closest animal relatives, and are some of the most intelligent animals. They live in tropical rain forests and woodlands in Africa. Chimps eat fruits, leaves, and seeds, but they also like termites and ants.

△ Chimps sometimes use twigs to pry insects out of their mounds, and will crack nuts open by hitting them with stones.

Fact box

• The tallest male chimps are about 5 feet tall when they stand up—about as big as a small human adult. Female chimps are shorter.
• Chimps can live to be 60 years old.
• Chimps live in groups. These have between 15 and 80 members.

△ Chimps spend a lot of their time in trees. They use their long arms to swing from branch to branch in search of food. At night, they build nests of leaves to sleep in.

◁ Chimps usually move around on all fours, but they can also walk upright, which leaves their hands free. If attacked, a chimp may defend itself by throwing stones.

Find out more
Baboon
Gorilla
Lemur
Monkey
Orangutan

Cobra

Cobras are poisonous snakes found in Africa, India, and Asia. The most deadly cobras are the mambas of Africa. A bite from a mamba will kill unless the victim is given antivenin (an antidote to snake venom) very quickly. Many people die each year from cobra bites.

Fact box

• Cobras eat small vertebrates (creatures with backbones).
• The black mamba moves as fast as a running human.
• Cobra venom stops the heart and lungs from working.

△ The king cobra is found in areas stretching from southern China to Indonesia. Reaching 18 feet in length, it is the world's longest poisonous snake. The female king cobra lays up to 40 eggs.

▷ In India, snake charmers catch common cobras. They play a tune on a pipe and the cobra rises up from the basket to "dance."

▽ One of the cobra's main predators is the mongoose. Mongooses move very quickly and can avoid getting bitten. When frightened, the cobra rears up and spreads its hood.

Find out more

Lizard
Rattlesnake
Reptile

Communication

Animals communicate with each other for many reasons—to find a mate, to warn of danger, or to scare other creatures away. They have many different ways of sending these signals to each other.

friendly   playful

ready to defend   ready to attack

◁ Wolves communicate using facial expressions. These four expressions carry very different messages.

△ Fireflies are beetles that use light to send signals. The light comes from special cells in their abdomens. The fireflies flash their lights to attract mates and to warn off predators.

▽ To hoot like an owl, clasp your hands together and blow between your thumbs. Do it outside at night, and an owl might hoot back at you.

△ Moths communicate using smell. The female gives off a scent and the male picks it up using his feathery antennae.

Find out more
Beetle
Butterfly and Moth
Owl
Wolf

Conservation

Many animals are in danger of dying out, or becoming extinct. This may be because their habitat has been destroyed or polluted, or because they have been hunted. It is important for us to conserve these animals and their homes.

△ Litter pollutes the environment. It is also dangerous to animals, who may get trapped inside empty cans and bottles. Collecting litter is an excellent way of helping animals.

△ Many corn crakes die when farmers cut their fields. New harvesting methods are now helping them survive.

◁ Dodos once lived on the island of Mauritius, but because they could not fly they were easily hunted by sailors visiting the island. In 1680, the dodo became extinct.

▽ In the last 50 years, the survival of whales has been threatened by overhunting. Nowadays, whale hunting is carefully controlled.

Find out more

Bison and Musk ox

Panda

Tiger

Whale

Coral reef

Coral reefs are found in shallow tropical seas. They look like underwater gardens, but the corals are not flowers—they are huge groups of tiny animals called polyps and their skeletons.

△ Coral reefs can stretch for thousands of miles. The biggest of all is the Great Barrier Reef off the coast of northeast Australia.

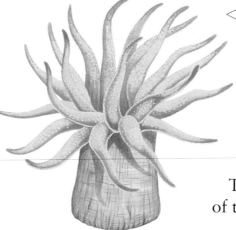

▽ A coral reef is home to an amazing variety of animals, from the conger eel and giant clam (bottom left) to the striped angelfish and coral-eating parrotfish above them. The reef gives them shelter from predators and is the source of food.

◁ A coral polyp has tentacles covered with stinging cells, which it uses to stun any tiny creature that passes by. As it grows, the polyp builds a cuplike skeleton around itself. When it dies, this is the only thing that remains. The reef is made of millions of these tiny skeletons.

Find out more
Eel
Seahorse
Shellfish
Starfish

Cow and Bull

Female cattle are called cows, and the males are called bulls. They are kept on farms all over the world for their meat, called beef, and for their milk. We also use their hides (skin) to make leather shoes and clothes.

Friesian cow

Jersey cow

Hereford bull

Highland cow

△ Female cattle that are reared for their milk are called dairy cows. Twice a day they are brought in from the fields to be milked. Special machines suck the milk from the cow's udder.

△ Although they are not smart animals, cattle are very strong. In many parts of the world, they are used to pull plows and carts.

△ There are over 250 breeds of cattle, and each has its own qualities. Friesians give a lot of milk. Jerseys are famous for their rich, creamy milk. Herefords are often used as beef cattle. Highland cattle are tough enough to survive cold winters.

Find out more
Bison and Musk ox
Buffalo
Pig
Sheep

Crab

Crabs are creatures with ten legs and a hard shell. Most live in the sea or along the shore, where they scurry sideways. Their two front legs are frightening pincers, used for getting food and fighting off attackers.

△ Hermit crabs do not have their own shells, but live in the empty shells of sea snails and whelks. As a hermit crab grows, it moves into bigger shells.

▽ Tropical horseshoe crabs are a very ancient species, related to spiders and scorpions. They emerge from the sea in large numbers to lay eggs on the shore.

◁ The legs of some crabs are adapted for swimming. The back legs of this swimmer crab are flattened like tiny paddles.

▷ Fiddler crabs live in muddy mangrove swamps in all regions of the world. One of the male fiddler crab's claws is huge. He waves it to attract females to his burrow.

Find out more
Lobster and Crayfish
Scorpion
Spider

Cricket and Grasshopper

Crickets and grasshoppers are insects that would rather hop on their long back legs than fly. Males "sing" to attract mates—grasshoppers do this by rubbing their back legs together, while crickets use their wings.

△ Many grasshoppers are brightly colored. This warns predators that the grasshopper can spit a nasty-tasting protective foam.

◁ Grasshoppers have very strong muscles in their long back legs, and they also have a remarkable spring in their knees. The grasshopper can jump 12 times its own length—this would be like a child jumping over a house!

△ Locusts are a kind of grasshopper found in Africa. Every now and then they form huge swarms, which destroy crops.

▽ Bush crickets, like this great green bush cricket, are known as katydids because the male's song sounds like someone saying, "Katy did." Females have slitlike ears in their front legs, which they use to listen to the singing males.

Fact box
• Crickets and grasshoppers eat leaves and grasses. Some eat other insects too.
• Each species has its own special song.
• People used to keep crickets in cages to hear them sing.

Find out more
Beetle
Dragonfly and Damselfly
Insect

Deep-sea fish

Down at the bottom of the ocean, the water is cold and dark. Food is scarce, and fish here must prey on one another or eat dead fish. Deep-sea fish are fairly small, but they often have huge, gaping jaws and stretchy stomachs to make the most of any food around.

▷ The gulper can completely unhinge its huge jaws so it can swallow larger fish. It also has a stomach that expands to deal with the largest of meals.

▽ Tubeworms called riftia live in the hot waters gushing from volcanic vents on the ocean floor. They eat bacteria that feed on sulfur from the hot vents.

Fact box
• Tripod fish stand on three long fins, waiting for their prey.
• If attacked, some deep-sea fish create flashes of light.
• Many deep-sea fish are totally blind.

▽ Like many fish in the dark depths, the anglerfish makes its own light. The female anglerfish's light dangles on a long stalklike fin in front of her mouth, to lure prey into her jaws. The male has no "fishing fin" and relies on the female to eat. He bites into her and feeds on her blood.

anglerfish

gulper eel

dragonfish

riftia

◁ Dragonfish have eyes, but they find their food in the dark by waving their long feelers through the water.

Find out more
Eel
Fish
Flatfish
Shark

Deer

Deer come in all shapes and sizes, from the tiny pudu to the large moose. They are graceful mammals that can run swiftly from danger. Deer are found in the Northern Hemisphere and South America.

△ **1** Make a cast of a deer hoofprint to keep forever. First take a piece of cardboard 2 or 3 inches wide and 20 inches long. Bend the cardboard into a circle around the hoofprint and fasten with tape.

△ **2** Mix some plaster of Paris powder with water to make a thick paste. Pour the paste into the cardboard mold until it reaches just below the top of the cardboard.

△ Each year, male deer grow a new set of antlers. During the breeding season, they fight fierce battles with each other to become leader of the herd.

△ **3** Leave it until it hardens, then carefully lift off the plaster in its mold. Take your cast home and remove the cardboard. Using an old toothbrush, clean off any soil from the plaster cast.

Find out more
Antelope
Elk
Mammal
Reindeer

Defense

A fast animal can run away from a predator, but slower animals need other methods of defense. Thick armor and sharp spines will deter many attackers, as will nasty poisons and bright colors. Other animals just hide and hope for the best!

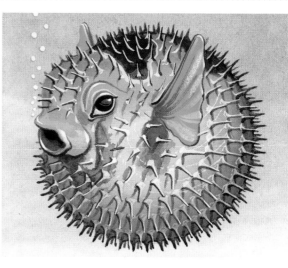

△ The porcupinefish puffs up its body to make its spines stand out. This will warn off most attackers.

◁ The octopus hides in a hole and changes color to blend into the rock. If spotted, it spreads out its tentacles to make itself look huge and frightening.

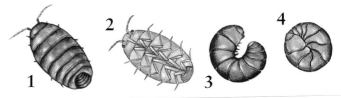

△ The wood louse defends itself by rolling into a ball so its tough, outer body is all an enemy can see.

▷ A game of hide-and-seek is a lot like a hunt between a predator and its prey. The hider will try to make herself as small as possible so that the seeker does not see or hear her.

Fact box

• Animals with a sting or poison often have red (or yellow) and black stripes. Predators learn to leave them alone.
• Lots of animals use camouflage to hide.

△ A shell acts like a coat of armor for a turtle. When danger threatens, it pulls its head and legs inside the shell until it is safe to come out.

Find out more
Armadillo
Baby animal
Camouflage
Turtle and Tortoise

Dog (domestic)

Dogs were domesticated about 12,000 years ago, when cavemen first tamed the Asiatic wolf. Since then, dogs have lived with people wherever they have traveled. Over time they have been bred to help people both in their everyday lives and in their work.

Bernese mountain dog

▷ There are about 400 dog breeds, which are divided into seven groups. These are: sporting dogs; hounds; working dogs; terriers; toy dogs; non-sporting dogs; and herding dogs. The Bernese mountain dog is a working dog, the Labrador retriever is a sporting dog, and the Yorkshire terrier is a toy dog.

Labrador retriever

Yorkshire terrier

▽▷ The collie (below) and the corgi (right) are both herding dogs. Collies help round up sheep. Corgis once helped herd cattle. Many collies work on farms, but most corgis are now just pets.

△ Dogs kept as pets should be taught to walk on a leash and housebroken. They must be properly cared for throughout their lives.

Find out more
Cat (domestic)
Dog (wild)
Fox
Hyena
Wolf

Dog (wild)

In many ways wild dogs look and behave like domestic dogs, and they are related. However, wild dogs are usually afraid of humans and cannot be trained. These meat-eaters often live in packs and are found all over the world.

▷ Like most wild dogs, the Cape hunting dogs of East Africa are fierce killers. They have long front teeth for piercing or tearing, and sharp cheek teeth for slicing meat into small chunks. They work in teams to chase down antelope, zebra, and wildebeest.

◁ Wild dogs rely on their sense of smell and sharp hearing for hunting. Once they have found their prey's scent, they give chase. Like other dogs, North American coyotes (left) howl to call up the pack for a hunt.

Fact box
- The dhole of India can kill bears and even tigers.
- Golden jackals of southeastern Europe now live mostly on humans' trash.
- The coyote is sometimes called the prairie wolf.

◁ Jackals live in Africa and Asia. They hunt mainly alone at night, and form packs only when there is a chance of sharing a lion's kill.

Find out more
Dog (domestic)
Fox
Wolf

48

Dolphin

Dolphins are intelligent, graceful sea creatures. They are not fish, but mammals and, like us, they breathe air. They make clicking sounds to help them find their way, catch their prey, and communicate.

white-sided dolphin

△ There are over 30 species of dolphin, found in seas all over the world.

Fact box
• A dolphin's top speed is 25 miles per hour.
• A dolphin breathes through a blowhole in the top of its head.

spotted dolphin

◁ Dolphins send out sounds in pulses. Then they listen for echoes reflected back from nearby objects to find out what is around them. This way, they can track down fish to eat.

▽ Bottle-nosed dolphins love to play. Like many other dolphin species, their streamlined shape and powerful tails help them speed through the water and they often jump high into the air. They live in big family groups called schools, and like to race alongside boats.

bottle-nosed dolphin

Find out more
Killer whale
Whale

Donkey

Patient and strong, donkeys are used all over the world to carry people and freight. Their small feet and thick coats equip them for working in dry, rocky places. Because they are quiet animals and are gentle with children, donkeys are often kept as pets.

▽ Donkeys range in color from almost white to nearly black. They usually have two dark stripes running along their backs and across their shoulders. Unlike horses, only the ends of their tails have long hairs.

▽ Donkeys are descended from wild asses that were tamed by the ancient Egyptians. Wild asses look very similar to donkeys, with large pointed ears and small hooves. They have thin black stripes on their legs, unlike donkeys.

▽ Donkeys are usually good workers. They can also be stubborn and will make a loud braying noise if they are angry or upset.

Find out more

Horse
Zebra

Dragonfly and Damselfly

Dragonflies are the fastest flying insects, swooping over the streams and ponds where they live at up to 55 miles per hour. Damselflies are thinner and more delicate, with a slow, fluttering flight.

△ Dragonflies and damselflies live near water. The young, called nymphs, hatch from eggs laid on plants. They feed on other water creatures, and after two years the nymphs grow into adults.

▷ The wings of the damselfly are almost transparent. They shimmer as the damselfly searches for small insects to eat.

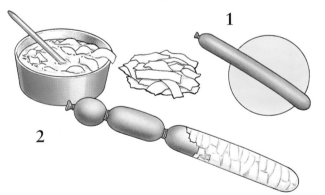

△ **1** To make a model dragonfly, start by blowing up a long balloon. **2** Twist and tie the balloon twice to make the three body sections, then cover the balloon with several layers of papier-mâché. When this is dry, paint the body.

▷ **3** Make the wings from wire bent into shape. Cover them with plastic wrap, then attach them to the body with some more wire. Attach pipe cleaners or straws to the middle section for the legs. For the eyes, cut a ping-pong ball in half and glue it to the head.

Find out more

Ant and Termite
Bee and Wasp
Beetle
Fly
Insect

Duck and Goose

Ducks and geese are water birds. Members of this family live in most parts of the world. They have thick plumage (feathers) to keep them warm, and webbed feet for paddling along in water.

△ Geese are generally bigger than ducks and have longer necks. Geese have big beaks for pulling up and eating grass. Ducks have flatter beaks for sifting food from the water.

◁ Ducks have short legs, and they waddle when they walk. Their feet have three front toes in a web and a rear toe that is free. Almost all duck species live in fresh water. Besides feeding on insects and worms, they eat vegetable matter.

△ Eider ducks breed along icy northern coasts. To keep her eggs warm, the female lines the nest with fluffy feathers (down) plucked from her breast.

▽ Most Canada geese that breed in Canada and Alaska migrate to Mexico and the southern United States in the winter. When they fly, they often make a honking noise.

△ Male ducks are called drakes. They often have colorful plumage, which is designed to attract females. Female ducks are usually dull brown.

Find out more
Bird
Gull
Migration
Pelican
Swan

Eagle

Strong wings, sharp eyes, and powerful talons make eagles great hunters. Their large, hooked bills are used for slicing open and eating— not for killing. They also scavenge if they find dead animals. These big birds of prey are found in regions from the Arctic to the tropics.

◁ The golden eagle (left) and the white-tailed sea eagle are the most widespread eagle species. They are found in Europe and northern Asia. Like most eagles, they nest on cliffs, raising one or two chicks a year.

△ The North American bald eagle is the national bird of the United States. It is not really bald, but has contrasting white head and brown body feathers. It lives close to lakes, rivers, and coasts.

Fact box

• Because they are so strong, eagles have been symbols of war and national power for thousands of years.

• Eagles mate for life and return to use the same nest every year.

▷ Harpy eagles come from the jungles of South America and the South Pacific. They are powerful hunters, eating sloths, macaws, and monkeys. The great harpy eagle (right) is the largest eagle.

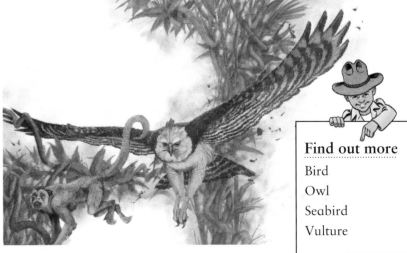

Find out more
Bird
Owl
Seabird
Vulture

Eel

Because they are long and thin, and have wriggly bodies, you may think that eels are a type of snake. In fact, they are fish. Like fish, they are scaly and have thin fins that run the length of their bodies.

▷ The moray eel can grow up to 10 feet long. It hides by day in holes in the rocks, and only comes out at night. It eats shellfish but will attack humans if disturbed.

▽ To breed, freshwater eels have to swim thousands of miles—from lakes and rivers in America and Europe, to the Sargasso Sea, near Bermuda. The eels' eggs hatch there and drift north in an ocean current. Up to three years later the young eels wriggle back into the rivers again.

Fact box

- Young eels are called elvers.
- There are about 600 kinds of eel, living in fresh and salt water all over the world.
- To reach lakes further inland, freshwater eels slither overland across damp grass.

△ The electric eel of South America eats small fish. It catches them by stunning the fish with an electric shock. This shock is so strong that it could knock down a human.

Find out more

Flatfish
Goldfish and Carp
Ray
Shellfish

Elephant

Elephants are the heaviest land animals. They are also intelligent and have good memories. There are two species: one lives in Africa, another in India. They use their long trunks almost like an arm, to put food and water in their mouths. Their tusks are made of ivory and males use them for fighting.

△ In India, elephants are trained to do heavy work, such as lifting logs. An elephant driver, or keeper, is called a mahout.

◁ **1** The African elephant is bigger than its Indian cousin. It has bigger tusks and ears and a hollow forehead. The tusks are really teeth that grow outside the mouth.

◁ **2** The Indian elephant has smaller ears and a rounded forehead. Only the male Indian elephant has tusks.

▽ In Africa, elephants live in small family groups ruled by the oldest females. Males live in all-male herds.

1

2

Fact box

• African elephants grow to 13 feet, over twice as tall as an adult human.
• They can weigh over 7 tons—heavier than six cars.
• Elephants can live to be 70.

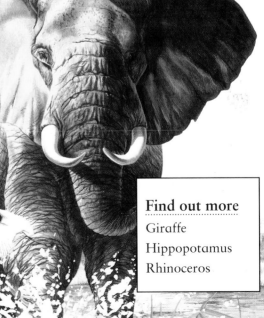

Find out more
Giraffe
Hippopotamus
Rhinoceros

Elk

There are two kinds of elk. One lives in Canada and the United States; the other lives in northern Europe and looks like the American moose. They are both large members of the deer family.

△ The American elk is known as a wapiti. Wapiti are closely related to the red deer of Europe. Like all deer, wapiti mainly eat fresh shoots and fruit.

▷ European elk are usually born as twins in the spring. They are unsteady on their feet at first, but are soon able to trot at a fast pace.

▷ Wapiti calves are born in the spring. Their white-spotted coats act as camouflage and help them hide from wolves and pumas.

◁ Male European elk, like American moose, grow huge spoon-shaped antlers. They use them to challenge other males and show off to the females. The older the male, the larger his antlers. The mating season in the fall is called the rut. At this time, male elks fill the air with low, grunting noises.

Find out more
Deer
Mammal
Reindeer

Evolution

Millions of years have passed since life first started on Earth. The animals that lived then are very different from those that are found now. This is because things evolve (change) over time to stand a better chance of survival.

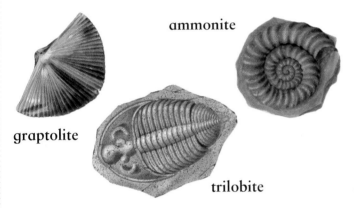

ammonite

graptolite

trilobite

△ **1** Fossils are the remains of animals that died millions of years ago. They are a good way of telling how things have evolved. You can find fossils on some beaches and in certain types of rock formations.

△ **2** Look at fossils with a magnifying glass. You will see that they look fairly similar to some animals still alive today. The way they have changed shows how they have evolved in order to survive.

◁ Once there was just one type of fox, but new forms evolved. The Arctic fox has thick fur to keep warm, and is colored white for camouflage.

▷ The desert fox has evolved to deal with the hot desert. It has large ears to help it keep cool, and is sandy in color.

◁ The peppered moth has evolved very recently. Usually this moth is light-colored but a black-winged form is found in places where the trees have been blackened by smoke from factories. This gives it better camouflage.

Find out more
Bird
Camouflage
Defense
Habitat

Fish

Fish live in salt water and fresh water all over the world. They are many different shapes and sizes, but almost all fish are covered with scales and have strong fins for swimming.

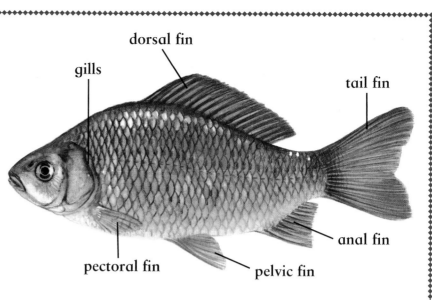

gills

dorsal fin

tail fin

anal fin

pectoral fin

pelvic fin

▷ Like us, fish need oxygen to live. But instead of breathing air, they absorb the oxygen in water. Water enters their mouths and is swept over the gills. The oxygen passes from the water straight into tiny blood vessels in the gills.

water out

water in

▽ Fish often swim in groups called schools. One reason they do this is for safety. Many fish together can confuse a predator, making it hard to single out one fish to attack.

▽ 1 A fish's scales lie in the same direction to help the fish slip easily through water. See how scales work by cutting out strips of paper and sticking them in layers onto a cardboard fish.

1

2

△ 2 Now run your hand over the paper scales from head to tail, and then from tail to head. It should feel very different.

Find out more
Deep-sea fish
Flatfish
Sharks

Flamingo, Heron, and Stork

Flamingos live in colonies on shallow lakes in Africa, South America, and Asia. They are pink with large wings, slim necks, and long, thin legs for wading in water. The largest is the great flamingo, which is 5 feet tall. Flamingos, herons, and storks are all in the same group of birds.

▽ Herons are long-legged like flamingos. They wade along the edges of lakes and rivers, hunting for fish. When they spot one, they spear it with their sharp beak. Like most wading birds, they often stand on one leg. This keeps the leg out of the water warm.

▽ Storks are also wading birds. White storks spend the winter in Africa, and in the summer fly to Europe to breed. Many Europeans think storks bring good luck. They build platforms on their chimneys so the birds can make their nests on them.

△ Flamingos wade through the shallows moving their heads from side to side. Their specially shaped beaks act like strainers, filtering shrimp and other tiny animals from the muddy water. Flamingos get their pink color from the shrimp they eat.

Find out more
Duck and Goose
Pelican
Swan

Flatfish

Flatfish are found in all of the world's oceans and seas. They range in weight and size from the huge Atlantic halibut to the small species of sole. They nestle on the ocean floor waiting for their prey—shellfish or smaller fish.

Fact box
- The Atlantic halibut grows to 6.5 feet in length and can weigh 715 pounds.
- Some flatfish change color to match the ocean floor. This hides them while they lie in wait for food.

▽ Anglerfish are flatfish that live on the ocean floor. They are covered in lumps and flaps that act as camouflage as they lie in wait among the seaweed and rocks. Like fishermen, they lure their prey with a rod, and as soon as it is close the small fish is snapped up.

△ Like all flatfish, the flounder family are colored on their upper side and white on their underside. Flounder have their eyes on the upper side of their heads.

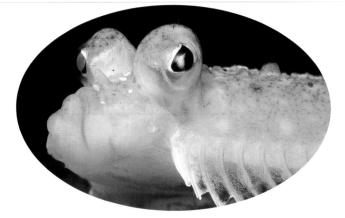

△ Young flatfish are born with an eye on either side of the head. As they grow, one eye moves to the same side of the head as the other eye. Meanwhile, the body and skull flatten out, and the mouth moves to the same side as the eyes.

Find out more
Deep-sea fish
Fish
Ray
Shellfish

Fly

There are many types of flies, and they are found everywhere. Unlike other insects, they have just one pair of wings for flying; their tiny back wings are only used for balance. A few flies carry deadly diseases, but many help plants by carrying pollen from one flower to another.

△ The African tsetse fly carries a disease called sleeping sickness. It spreads the disease from wild animals to humans and livestock by biting them and drinking their blood.

Fact box

- House flies beat their wings 200 times a second.
- Gnats beat their wings 1,000 times a second. This is what makes the buzzing sound common to all flies.

△ The hover fly, also called the flower fly, gets its name from the fact that it hovers around flowers. Hover flies have markings like wasps.

▽ Like all flies, dung flies spend the first part of their lives as maggots. During this time, they live inside the dung left by animals. They feed on the dung and, in doing so, clear it up.

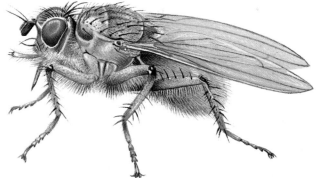

◁ Bluebottles (left) and house flies feed on all kinds of food. They have "taste buds" on their feet. These tell them whether something they have landed on is good to eat.

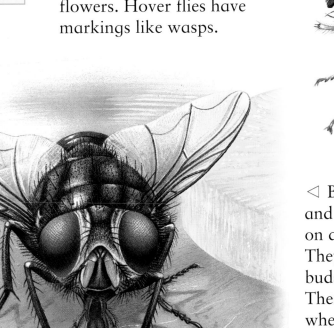

Find out more
Ant and Termite
Bee and Wasp
Beetle
Insect

Food

All animals need to eat in order to survive. Animals that eat plants are called herbivores; those that eat meat are carnivores. A chain of living things that eat each other is called a food chain.

◁ **1** A mobile is a good way of showing how a food chain works. Cut out shapes of an owl, a mouse, and a lump of grain from pieces of colored cardboard.

▷ **2** The mouse eats the grain and the owl eats the mouse. So hang the grain inside the mouse, and the mouse inside the owl. Connect the shapes with pieces of string.

△ This puma has killed a deer. Once the puma has eaten its fill, the remains will be food for vultures, ravens, coyotes, and maggots.

▷ There are many different food chains. One food chain in the ocean starts with phytoplankton. These tiny plants make their food from sunshine.

phytoplankton

copepods

herring

cod

△ Nothing is wasted in a food chain. Even the smallest scraps of dead animal will be food for another creature.

killer whale

harbor seal

◁ Each animal is eaten by a bigger one. The killer whale is at the top of this particular food chain. So, indirectly, it gets its food from the tiny phytoplankton.

Find out more
Defense
Killer whale
Microscopic animal
Puma

Fox

Foxes are small wild dogs with short legs and big, bushy tails. They are skillful hunters that come out at night and rest by day in burrows called dens. The female is called a vixen, the male is a dog, and the young are cubs.

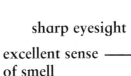

good hearing ———

sharp eyesight ———

excellent sense ——— of smell

△ The red fox lives in woodland and feeds on small animals, insects, and fruit. Foxes living near towns may scavenge from trash cans.

◁ Foxes are found in most parts of the world. The fennec fox lives in the deserts of North Africa and Arabia. During the day it stays below ground in its burrow to avoid the heat of the sun. Its huge ears also help it lose heat and keep cool.

▷ Foxes' pointed ears give them very good hearing. This helps them detect the slightest noise of a small animal in the grass. Roll two pieces of cardboard into cones and hold them to your ears. Get a friend to make a noise behind you, then hear for yourself the difference with the cones and without.

Find out more

Dog (domestic)
Dog (wild)
Wolf

Frog and Toad

Frogs and toads are amphibians, so they live both in water and on land. Frogs have moist skins, but toads are normally dry. While frogs use their strong back legs for jumping, toads walk. They are both good swimmers.

△ The female Surinam toad has special pockets on her back in which her eggs grow. After 80 days, the young toads emerge from the pockets.

△ Many tropical frogs are brightly colored. This warns other animals that they are poisonous. The poison of the South American poison dart frog (bottom) is so strong that native people put it on the tips of their arrows.

▷ 1 Most frogs and toads lay their eggs, called spawn, in water. 2 After two weeks, tadpoles hatch. 3 Like fish, they breathe through gills, but gradually grow legs. 4 After three months, the gills shrink, the tail gets short, and the lungs develop. 5, 6 The tiny frogs are able to leave the water and grow into adults on land.

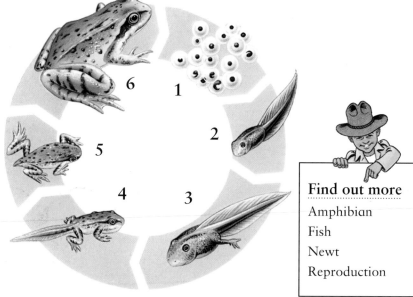

Find out more

Amphibian
Fish
Newt
Reproduction

Giraffe

Giraffes are the world's tallest animals, measuring up to 20 feet. Their front legs are so long that they have to spread them wide apart in order to drink at water holes.

▽ Giraffes live in small family groups on the African plains. About 15 months after mating, the female giraffe gives birth to a calf. The calf can get up on its feet and follow its mother only an hour or two after being born.

◁ The spotted pattern on its coat helps hide the giraffe from its enemies. Spots can be big (above), or blotchy (left). Each giraffe has a different pattern.

△ Giraffes use their height to graze on the leaves at the top of acacia thorn trees. The giraffe tears off the spiky twigs in its tough mouth. It can also curl its long tongue around even higher branches and pull them down to its mouth.

Find out more

Antelope
Buffalo
Zebra

Goat

Hardy and good at climbing, goats can survive in the highest mountains. Wild goats are found across the Northern Hemisphere. Tame goats are kept for their milk, meat, and skin.

△ Kashmir and Angora goats are valued for their fine wool. The long, silky coat of the Angora (above) gives mohair or angora wool. Kashmir goats give cashmere wool.

feral goat

Cretan wild goat

Apennine mountain goat

△ Goats were first tamed 10,000 years ago, and there are now many breeds. They like to eat grass and plants, but they will eat almost anything and can survive on thorn trees and shrubs. Male goats are often bad-tempered and use their long, curved horns to fight each other for females.

▽ Ibexes are wild goats found in Europe, Africa, and Asia. They live on the mountaintops in the summer, and move to warmer lower pastures in the winter.

Fact box
- Goats' hooves have hard edges and soft centers. They act like suction cups on slippery rocks.
- Goats give off a very strong smell.
- A young goat is a called a kid, a female is a doe or a nanny, and a male is a billy.

Find out more
Antelope
Cow and Bull
Sheep
Yak

Goldfish and Carp

Goldfish and carp originally came from lakes and streams in Asia and were first introduced into the United States in the late 1800s. Goldfish are often small and brightly colored; carp are larger and usually have plainer coloring.

common goldfish

comet

△ Goldfish survive well in both outdoor ponds and indoor tanks. They come in a wide range of colors and shapes.

silver carp

△ Carp are found in North America, Asia, and Europe. Grass carp are helpful to humans because they eat pondweed. In China, the silver carp is bred for food.

△ **1** Taking care of goldfish is easy. You will need a tank with clean gravel and a few large objects. You should also put in some water plants to give the fish oxygen to breathe.

▷ **2** Fill the tank with water and carefully place the goldfish in the tank. You will need to feed them daily, and you must be sure to clean the tank and change the water regularly.

Find out more
Eel
Fish
Flatfish
Salmon and Trout

Gorilla

Gorillas are huge and powerful apes. They look fierce, but are actually gentle vegetarians. They are now very rare and are found only in the forests and mountains of Central Africa.

▽ Gorillas live in family groups. These are led by a big male called a silverback, who gets his name from the silver hairs on his back. These hairs grow when a male gorilla is about ten years old. Silverbacks may be as tall as a man and weigh 500 pounds—about three times as much as a man.

△ Gorillas eat leaves and buds, stalks, berries, and sometimes even tree bark. When they have eaten most of the food in one place, they move on to let the plants grow back again.

◁▽ Gorillas learn to walk at about ten months. They feed on their mother's milk for the first two years and spend much of their time playing. They sleep with their mothers until they are three years old, then they make their own nests of leaves and branches.

Find out more
Baboon
Chimpanzee
Monkey
Orangutan

Guinea pig, Gerbil, and Hamster

Guinea pigs, gerbils, and hamsters are all mammals. These rodents live wild in many parts of the world, but they also make very good pets. They need a good-sized cage and should be given food and water every day. They also enjoy lots of care and attention.

Fact box

• Hamsters are originally from Europe and Asia; guinea pigs, from South America; and gerbils, from Africa and Asia.
• Guinea pigs were taken to Europe as long ago as the 1500s.
• Despite their name, guinea pigs are not related to pigs.

▽ In South America, humans have been eating guinea pig meat for about 4,000 years. Wild guinea pigs, called cavies, still live on the grasslands there.

△ Guinea pigs feed on grass and green plants in the wild, so if you give them dry pet food, make sure they have plenty of water.

▽ Hamsters live alone and come out at night to eat grasses, seeds, and berries. They have big pouches in their cheeks that they use to carry food back to their nests.

▷ Gerbils live on the edges of hot deserts. They hide in burrows by day and come out at night to feed on seeds and insects. Their long back legs and tails help them leap across the hot, sandy ground.

Find out more

Beaver
Mouse
Rabbit and Hare
Rat
Squirrel

Gull

Gulls, or seagulls, are large, sturdy seabirds with webbed feet. There are over 40 species, found in coastal areas all over the world. Sometimes gulls are found inland, in the countryside, and in towns and cities.

△ Gulls eat many different foods, including fish, eggs, earthworms, and insects. They also scavenge for food in garbage dumps.

▽ Baby gulls are covered in soft, fluffy feathers, called down. They are fed by their parents until the chicks have grown their flight feathers.

▽ Gulls are strong fliers, soaring and gliding on the strong sea breezes. Many gulls nest on cliffs, forming large and noisy colonies.

▽ Parents often have to fend off other gulls, like the lesser black-backed gull, that try to eat eggs and chicks from their nests.

Find out more
Albatross
Bird
Duck and Goose
Puffin
Seabird

Habitat

A habitat is the place where an animal lives. It provides the animal with food, water, and shelter—everything it needs to survive. There are many different habitats all over the world.

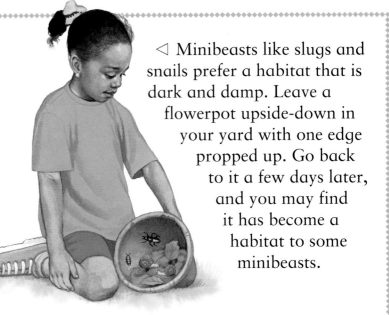

◁ Minibeasts like slugs and snails prefer a habitat that is dark and damp. Leave a flowerpot upside-down in your yard with one edge propped up. Go back to it a few days later, and you may find it has become a habitat to some minibeasts.

savanna

rain forest

desert

△ Over time, animals have evolved to survive in their own habitats. For example, the camel is able to live in the desert because it can go for days without drinking. If a habitat changes—for example, if the rainfall decreases—each animal must adapt to the new environment. Unlike humans, if an animal is suddenly taken out of its habitat it cannot adapt quickly enough and is unlikely to survive.

Find out more
Camel
Chimpanzee
Evolution
Giraffe

Hedgehog

Hedgehogs are mammals found in the woods and hedges of Europe, Asia, and Africa. Most have thousands of thick spines covering their backs, which help protect them from predators. There are also hairy hedgehogs, which live in Asia.

▽ The common hedgehog usually has about four babies. The babies do not get stung when they drink their mother's milk, because she only has spines on her back. Adults go out after dark to hunt for food. They will eat plants, but prefer insects and frogs.

Fact box

• Babies are born blind, with soft spines.
• Hedgehogs spend more than 20 hours a day sleeping. In cold northern regions, they hibernate in the winter, curling up under a pile of leaves.
• One hedgehog, the moon rat of Sumatra, can be 16 inches long.

△ Hedgehogs can be friendly, especially if you leave them some dog or cat food. It is best not to touch them, though, as they often carry fleas.

△ When a hedgehog senses danger, it curls up into a tight ball with its spines on the outside. This discourages most predators, although many hedgehogs are killed by cars when they curl up on roads. They are able to climb trees, and if they fall, the spines act as a cushion.

Find out more
Fox
Mole
Porcupine
Weasel

Hippopotamus

These huge animals have large barrel-shaped bodies and short legs. The name hippopotamus comes from Greek and means "river horse." Although they are not related to horses, they do live near rivers—in Africa.

▷ Hippos spend the day in the water with just their eyes, nose, and ears showing. This stops them from getting sunburned. They can stay underwater for up to ten minutes before having to come up for air.

Fact box
- Hippos live in groups of up to 15 in rivers, lakes, and ponds across Africa.
- They can grow to 15 feet long, stand 5 feet at the shoulder, and weigh as much as 5 tons.
- Hippos are related to pigs.

△ Hippos have gigantic mouths with two huge tusks on the bottom jaw. In the breeding season, competing males show off the size of their mouths and may cut each other with their tusks. Hippos leave the water at night and travel to look for the grasses they eat. They have hard lips, which they use to cut the grass.

◁ Baby hippos can weigh 120 pounds at birth. They can stand within minutes of being born, and must stay close to their mother for protection.

Find out more
Horse
Pig
Rhinoceros

73

Horse

Long legs, a big heart, and large lungs make horses strong and fast—which is why people have used them to ride and to pull carts for 5,000 years. Horses are descended from wild horses that once lived on grassy plains in herds.

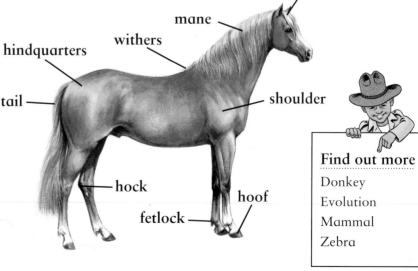

dun

dark bay

roan

light bay

palomino

piebald

chestnut

gray

skewbald

black

▷ Horses come in many colors, each with a special name.

◁ Ponies can be kept as family pets. They need a field to live in, and lots of care and attention. They should be exercised regularly and need their hooves trimmed every few weeks.

▽ Grooming keeps a pony's coat glossy and healthy. Be sure never to walk behind a horse or pony—it may kick out in surprise.

▽ Every part, or point, of a horse has a name. Horses are measured in hands. One hand is 4 inches—the average width of a man's hand.

forelock

mane

withers

hindquarters

tail

shoulder

hock

hoof

fetlock

Find out more

Donkey
Evolution
Mammal
Zebra

Hummingbird

When hummingbirds hover, their wings beat so fast that they hum, and this gives them their name. These tiny birds live in warm places in North and South America.

▽ Hummingbirds use their long beaks to reach the nectar deep inside flowers.

◁ Hummingbirds use up so much energy beating their wings that they need to feed often. The nectar they eat is full of sugar, which gives them energy quickly.

△ A hummingbird's wings swivel. This means it can hover at a flower while keeping its head perfectly still. It can also fly backward.

Fact box

• Ruby-throated hummingbirds fly 500 miles nonstop across the Gulf of Mexico when migrating.
• Hummingbirds normally lay two eggs, which are the smallest of any bird's.
• There are over 300 species of hummingbird.

▷ All hummingbirds are tiny, but the bee hummingbird of Cuba is the world's smallest bird. It is just 2 inches long— no bigger than a child's thumb.

Find out more
Bird
Migration
Ostrich
Sparrow

Hyena

Hyenas are mammals that live in Africa and Asia. They mainly eat the bones and flesh left by lions after a kill. Their jaws are so strong that they can crush and eat bones that even lions cannot handle.

striped hyena

brown hyena

△ Brown and striped hyenas are smaller and less fierce than spotted hyenas. They often prowl around at night, eating the remains of other animals' kills.

▷ Spotted hyenas are also known as laughing hyenas because of the weird cries they make. The largest and strongest of hyenas, they grow up to 6.5 feet long. Spotted hyenas hunt in packs and will sometimes attack rhinos.

◁ The aardwolf is a close relative of the hyena that lives in southern Africa. It is smaller than a hyena and eats only termites, ants, and insects.

Find out more
Dog (wild)
Fox
Lion
Wolf

Insect

There are more insects on Earth than any other group of creatures. There are probably more than a million species, and they live in almost every region and habitat in the world.

◁ Insects can carry out complicated tasks and will often build elaborate structures. Hornets, for example, build nests out of chewed-up wood or mud. They kill caterpillars and bring them back as food for their young.

Fact box
• The smallest insect is the fairy fly—just $^8/_{1000}$ inch long.
• Mayflies live just a few hours, but some beetles live many years.
• An ant can lift 50 times its own weight.
• Cockroaches can grow up to 4 inches long.

▷ All insects have six legs, a pair of antennae, and a body made of three parts: the head, the thorax, and the abdomen. The legs are always attached to the thorax. Insects are invertebrates, so instead of having bones, the body is encased in a tough shell. Many insects also have two pairs of wings.

antenna

thorax

head

leg

abdomen

◁ Many insects only come out at night. A good way to watch them on a summer evening is to hang a white sheet on a clothesline and to shine a flashlight at it. Moths and other flying insects will be attracted to the patch of light.

Find out more
Ant and Termite
Bee and Wasp
Beetle
Butterfly and Moth
Fly

Jellyfish

Jellyfish are sea creatures whose soft, wobbly bodies are made almost entirely of water. The smallest jellyfish are just a few inches in width, and the largest can be over 6 feet wide.

▽ The Australian box jellyfish stuns its prey with its poisonous tentacles. Then it pulls the creature toward its mouth, inside its bell-shaped body.

▽ The Portuguese man-of-war has a bag filled with gas on top of its body. As it floats above the water, the man-of-war trails its tentacles behind it. These tentacles can be up to 165 feet long and are a danger to swimmers as well as fish.

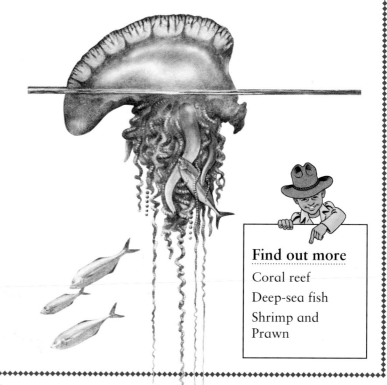

Fact box

- Many humans have been killed by the sting of the Australian box jellyfish.
- Jellyfish are invertebrates. This means that they have no spine (backbone).
- The largest jellyfish measured had tentacles 6 feet long.

△ Some types of jellyfish drift along wherever the ocean currents carry them. But others can propel themselves rapidly by pumping water out from folds in their bodies.

Find out more

Coral reef
Deep-sea fish
Shrimp and Prawn

Kangaroo and Wallaby

Kangaroos and wallabies live in Australia. They are marsupials. This means that the females have pouches on their bellies where their babies can grow until they are big enough to come out into the world.

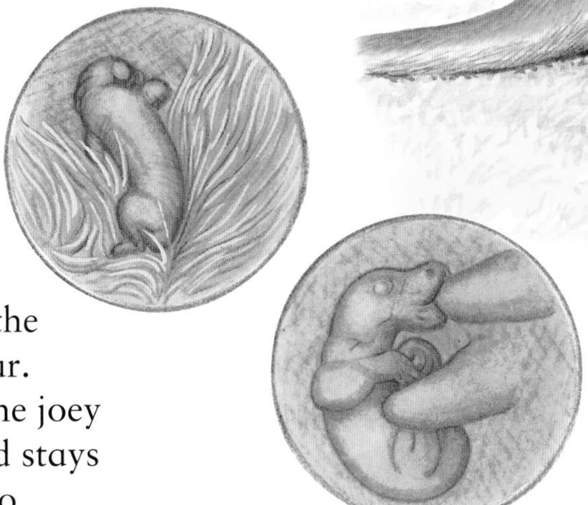

▷ A baby kangaroo is called a "joey." When it is born, the baby is less than an inch long. It crawls up to the mother's pouch along a path the mother licks in her fur. Once in the pouch, the joey clings to a nipple and stays there until it is able to take care of itself.

△ There are 56 species of kangaroo and wallaby (the name given to the smaller kangaroos). Most live on the ground, but some live in trees.

▷ Kangaroos are excellent jumpers. They bound along on their strong back legs, using their long tails for balance. They can jump over 30 feet in one leap.

Find out more
Koala, Wombat, and Opossum
Mammal
Platypus

Killer whale

Killer whales are the largest members of the dolphin family. They are powerful hunters and can be up to 33 feet in length. Killer whales have strong jaws and teeth. They eat fish, dolphins, seals— even other whales.

▽ Killer whales find their way and track their prey by sending out little clicks of sound, then picking up the echo. They live in families called pods. Usually there are ten or so in a pod, but there may be up to 100. Like all whales, killer whales are mammals and give birth to live young.

Fact box
• Killer whales sometimes launch themselves onto a beach to catch seals resting near the water line.
• One killer whale caught in the Bering Sea had 32 seals in its stomach.
• Killer whales have never killed, or even attacked, humans.

△ Killer whales are fast swimmers, with rounded flippers and strong tails. They can swim at over 37 miles per hour, and can jump high out of the water. They live in most of the world's oceans, near the North and South poles.

Find out more
Dolphin
Ray
Shark
Whale

Kiwi

Kiwis are birds that live in the thick forests of New Zealand. Many of these forests are being cut down, so kiwis are now rare. Kiwis have a long beak, short legs, and no tail. Their wings are too small for flying and are hidden under a coat of long, fine feathers.

Fact box

• Kiwis are the size of chickens and weigh about 9 pounds.
• A kiwi egg weighs about 1 pound and is nine times as big as a hen's egg.
• Kiwis are related to the giant moa, which is now extinct.

△ Kiwis mostly come out at night. In the daytime, they sleep in burrows in the earth. Kiwis can run very fast if threatened, and defend themselves with their claws.

△ Birds can usually see well, but the kiwi's eyesight is weak. However, unlike most birds, the kiwi has a very good sense of smell, and this helps it find food. Its nostrils are at the tip of the beak, and the kiwi uses its beak to search the ground for worms, insects, seeds, and berries.

▷ The kakapo also comes from New Zealand. Like the kiwi, it cannot fly, so it is easily caught by pet cats and dogs. It is now one of the world's rarest birds.

Find out more
Bird
Ostrich
Parrot
Penguin

Koala, Wombat, and Opossum

Koalas live in the eucalyptus forests of eastern Australia. Because they look a little like bears, they are sometimes called koala bears. However, they are marsupials, not bears. Wombats and opossums are also marsupials.

△ Wombats look like koalas, and also live in Australia. But they are larger—between 28 and 48 inches long—and live on the ground. During the day they stay in the grassy nests that they make at the end of their long burrows. They come out at night to feed on grasses and the roots of shrubs and trees.

▽ The only marsupials to live outside Australia are opossums, which are found in North and South America. A typical opossum grows to about 40 inches long. At least half its length is its hairless tail, which can grip things.

△ When a young koala leaves its mother's pouch, it rides on her back. Koalas spend all their lives up in eucalyptus trees eating the leaves and bark. They only come down to cross to another clump of trees.

Find out more

Kangaroo and Wallaby

Mammal

Platypus

Komodo dragon and Iguana

Komodo dragons are not really dragons and do not breathe fire. But they are 10 feet long—the biggest lizards alive. They live mainly on the Indonesian island of Komodo.

△ Iguanas, like this common iguana, are also big lizards, but they are smaller than Komodo dragons and live in North and South America. Common iguanas can grow up to 6 feet in length, and may have spines running along their backs.

◁ Komodo dragons eat carrion (rotting meat) and also hunt deer and wild pigs. They use their long, forked tongues to pick up the scent of their prey. They attack the animal with a short, fast sprint, and use their powerful jaws to rip it to pieces. Komodo dragons sometimes live to be 100 years old.

◁ The marine iguanas of the Galapagos Islands in the Pacific Ocean spend most of their lives beside the ocean. They feed on the seaweed and algae that grow below the water line, and can eat underwater for up to 20 minutes.

Find out more

Chameleon
Lizard
Newt

Lemur

Lemurs live only on the island of Madagascar and are rare because the forests where they live are being destroyed. Although they look like monkeys, lemurs belong to a different family.

▷ Most lemurs spend their time high up in the trees, but the ring-tailed lemur is often found on the ground. It is the only lemur to have a striped tail, which it uses to signal to other lemurs.

▽ The rare indri is the biggest lemur and may reach 4 feet tall. It is unusual because it comes out during the day and has only a tiny stump for a tail.

Fact box

• Lemurs are primates like apes, monkeys, and humans.
• Most lemurs eat fruit and leaves, as well as insects and eggs.
• The smallest lemur is the mouse lemur, at only 6 inches long. Most lemurs are around 24 inches.

△ Like most lemurs, the aye-aye is active at night, using its big eyes and ears to find food and sense danger. It has an extra-long middle finger on each front paw. It uses this to hook insects and grubs out of holes in trees and to spoon them into its mouth.

Find out more

Chimpanzee
Gorilla
Monkey
Orangutan

Leopard

Leopards are the most common of all the big cats. They live in forests, deserts, mountains, and grasslands, and are found in Africa, India, and Asia. They have become rarer in India and Asia because they have been hunted for their striking, spotted coats.

△ Leopards usually live alone, with males and females only getting together to mate. Females usually give birth to three cubs. Young cubs are carried by the scruff of the neck in their mother's mouth.

▷ Leopards are strong animals and good climbers. They carry prey up trees to keep it from scavengers. Leopards hunt gazelles, pigs, and monkeys, but they will eat birds and insects if there is nothing else to eat.

◁ Leopards are great swimmers and love being in water to play and to hunt. In wet areas, like highland and tropical forests, leopards have black fur. These leopards are called panthers.

Find out more
Cheetah
Lion
Mammal
Tiger

Lion

Lions are the largest predators in Africa. These powerful big cats live in groups called prides in bush country or on grassy plains. A pride is made up of several females and their cubs, as well as a few males. Except for humans, the lion has no enemies and is known as the "king of the beasts."

▽ Lions hunt mostly at night and spend the day resting. They prey on many of the large animals of the plains, including antelope, zebra, and buffalo. Besides caring for the cubs, the lionesses (female lions) do most of the hunting.

△ The male lion has a large, shaggy mane around its neck. It is his job to defend the territory of his pride, and he will warn off intruders with a loud roar. Adult lions have tawny coats, but lion cubs have spots.

Find out more
Cheetah
Leopard
Mammal
Puma
Tiger

Lizard

Lizards are reptiles. They have scaly skin, long tails, and usually live in warm countries. Although they can dart around very quickly, they are cold-blooded and need to lie in the sun to keep warm.

△ The Gila monster is a lizard that lives in the North American deserts. Bright red-and-black markings warn that it has a poisonous bite.

△ Many lizards turn darker when basking in the sun. This helps their bodies absorb its heat better.

△ The Australian thorny devil looks frightening, but it is harmless. Its sharp spines save it from being eaten by predators.

◁ The frilled lizard of Australia lifts up its huge neck collar to scare off attackers.

Fact box

• The smallest lizards, the geckos of the Virgin Islands, are 1.5 inches long.
• If some species of lizard are caught by the tail, the tail breaks off. A new one will grow in its place within eight months.

Find out more

Chameleon
Komodo dragon and Iguana
Newt

Llama

The llama is found in the high Andes mountains and on the dry plains of South America. Like its relative, the alpaca, it is tame. They are both relatives of the wild guanaco. All three are members of the camel family.

△ Guanacos usually live on mountains over 13,000 feet high, although they are also found on the lower plains. Their blood is rich in red cells, which helps them breathe the thin mountain air.

△ Today, llamas are used mainly as pack animals, as they were by the ancient Inca people of Peru. Female llamas are used for meat, but males are too tough to eat.

▷ Alpaca wool is prized by the local South American people. It has a soft feel and provides warmth in the cold climate.

Find out more
Camel
Goat
Mammal
Yak

Lobster and Crayfish

Lobsters and crayfish are water creatures with large claws and hard shells covering their bodies. Lobsters are found in oceans all over the world and can grow to be 20 inches long. Crayfish live in fresh water and are smaller.

△ Crayfish live in holes in the banks of rivers and lakes, or under stones. They hunt snails and insect larvae, and feed on dead or dying fish. They also eat water plants.

△ A lobster stalks across the ocean floor at night looking for food. It usually eats dead sea creatures, which it crushes in its giant claws. When frightened, it shoots backward by flicking its powerful tail.

▽ The spiny lobster is also called the crawfish. It has no large claws, and defends itself with its long antennae instead.

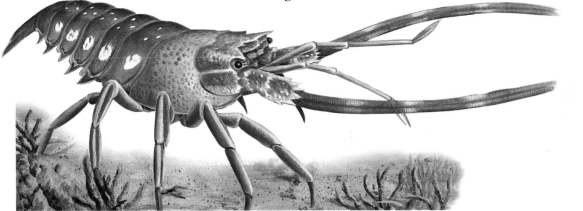

Find out more
Crab
Shellfish
Shrimp and
Prawn

Mammal

Mammals are a group of animals that includes humans. They are warm-blooded vertebrates and are found all over the world—in the water, in the air, and on land. There are 4,000 species of mammal, and they all have certain features in common.

△ A human and a cat are both mammals. They are each covered in hair or fur and both have a jawbone joint which only mammals have.

▽ All mammals feed their young on milk produced by the female. Except for animals such as the platypus, all mammals give birth to live young.

△ Mammals can be carnivores (meat-eaters), herbivores (plant-eaters), or omnivores (meat- and plant-eaters). This bush baby is an omnivore that belongs to a group of mammals called primates that can grasp objects with their hands.

▷ Because mammals are warm-blooded, they keep the same body temperature no matter how hot or cold the surroundings. Ask an adult to help you measure your temperature in a warm place and then in a cold place. It should always stay close to 98.6° F.

Find out more
Baby animal
Evolution
Rabbit and Hare
Reproduction

Meerkat

Meerkats are small meat-eating mammals. The word meerkat means "marsh cat." However, they actually live on the dry, open plains of Africa, not on marshes. They are known for their comic way of standing on their hind legs, on the lookout for predators.

△ Meerkats live in burrows under the ground. They come out during the day to hunt for food, but they are always watching out for eagles and other birds of prey.

▽ Meerkats often hunt by digging for prey with their long, sharp claws. They also look for insects, eggs, small animals, and plant roots to eat. They have a good sense of smell, and can see and hear well.

△ Like the meerkat, the mongoose will often attack poisonous snakes, in order to defend its burrow and its young.

Find out more
Cat (wild)
Cobra
Mammal
Weasel

Microscopic animal

Some animals are so tiny they can only be seen through a microscope. They live almost everywhere—in the water, in the air, in the ground, and even in your bed.

△ A good way to see microscopic animals is to look at pondwater through a microscope. Make a note of what you see as you look at the slide. You will probably see animals called daphnias, also known as water fleas.

Fact box

• There can be 5,000 house-dust mites on one speck of dust.
• Many people have tiny demodex mites living on their eyelashes.
• Some species of feather-winged beetle are as small as $1/1000$ inch in length.

△ Amoebas are among the tiniest living things. They move by changing shape.

▷ Zooplankton are tiny creatures that drift in water. They are the food of the world's biggest animal, the blue whale.

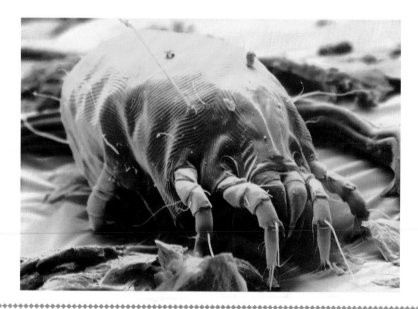

◁ House-dust mites are invisible to the naked eye. They feed on flakes of skin that they find in bedding and soft fabrics. These eight-legged creatures are related to spiders, and there are millions of them in each house.

Find out more
Beetle
Reproduction
Spider
Whale

Migration

Many animals make journeys from one place to another to find better living conditions. Some move fairly short distances, but others travel from one side of the world to the other. These regular return trips are known as migration.

▷ In the fall, you may see "V" formations of Canada geese flying overhead. Make a note of when they leave and in which direction they go. Watch for their return in the spring.

▽ The Earth is crisscrossed with animal migration routes. Use the color-keyed arrows on the map to see where these four migrating species travel each year.

■ Canada geese (above) fly to the Arctic Circle in the spring to breed. In the fall, they return to warmer southern regions.

■ Gray whales spend the winter in the warm sea off California, where they give birth to their calves. In the summer, they swim north to the rich food supplies in Alaskan waters.

■ Swifts spend the summer in Europe, where they catch insects to feed their young. They spend the winter in Africa.

■ Arctic terns travel farther than any other animal. Each year, they move from pole to pole and back again.

◁ Many grass-eating animals in Africa migrate to find food. Like these wildebeest, they follow the rain as it moves.

Find out more

Arctic tern
Reindeer
Swift and Swallow
Whale

Mole

Moles are small mammals that spend almost all their lives underground. We know they are around because of the molehills they create when digging their tunnels. They live in Europe, Asia, and North America.

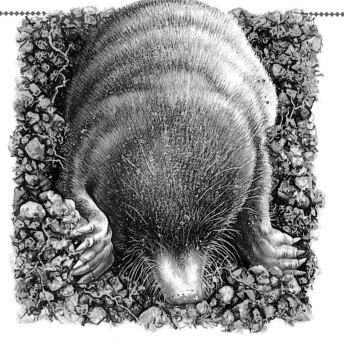

△ Big, powerful front paws, a pointed nose, and sharp claws mean that moles are excellent diggers. Although they have bad eyesight, they hunt for worms and insects by using their good sense of smell and by picking up vibrations with their whiskers.

△ Baby moles are born in a nest, called a fortress, deep below a molehill. They are lucky to be born at all—like all moles, their parents fought furiously when they first met.

◁ When moles dig tunnels they push the soil to the surface, which makes molehills. These are more common in the fall, when young moles look for new areas to live.

Fact box

- Moles surface at night to search for nest material.
- The star-nosed mole has a star of sensitive fleshy tentacles on its nose.
- People used to make clothes from mole fur.

◁ Golden moles are found in dry places in Africa. They live underground and burrow through sand to find food. Like all moles, they have very soft and silky coats.

Find out more
Badger
Mammal
Mouse
Worm

Monkey

Monkeys are intelligent mammals that can solve problems and hold things in their hands. They live in groups called troops, high in the tropical forests of the Americas, Africa, and Asia. Monkeys eat plants, birds' eggs, small animals, and insects.

△ A monkey's eyes face forward, which helps it see well when hunting. Most monkeys hunt by day.

△ Howler monkeys come from South America and are good climbers. They use their tails as an extra "hand" when swinging through the branches. Howler monkeys live in groups headed by an old male. They get their name from the loud calls the group makes together to warn other monkeys off their territory.

▷ The capuchin monkey is a small monkey that lives in the Amazon jungle. Because of its intelligence and curious nature, many have been kept as pets and taught to do tricks.

▽ The proboscis monkey of Borneo gets its name from its big nose. It has a long tail too, but uses it only for balance.

Fact box
- One difference between monkeys and apes is that monkeys have tails, while apes do not.
- A female monkey usually has one baby, or sometimes, twins.

Find out more
Baboon
Chimpanzee
Gorilla
Lemur
Orangutan

Mouse

Mice are small rodents with long tails and sharp front teeth. These grow all the time, so mice must gnaw things to stop them from getting too long. There are many kinds of wild mice, found all over the world. Mice can also be kept as pets.

△ American harvest mice are good at climbing. They build globe-shaped nests above the ground on the stems of grasses.

△ Mice eat many foods, including seeds, grain, roots, fruit, and insects. They also enjoy human food. The house mouse lives in people's homes.

▽ Test how smart your pet mouse is with this mouse-maze. Cut some cardboard into strips 6 inches wide, then glue the strips to a wooden board in a maze pattern. Put some food at the end of the maze and see how long your mouse takes to find it. Repeat to see if it gets quicker at solving the maze.

◁ Dormice live in Europe, Africa, and Asia. Unlike many other mice, they have furry tails. Dormice make nests from plants and, in cold places, sleep through the winter.

Find out more
Beaver
Food
Guinea pig, Gerbil, and Hamster
Rat

Newt

Newts are amphibians, so they can live both in water and on land. They begin their lives in the water, moving to the land as adults. Newts live in damp woods in Europe, Asia, and North America.

△ In the spring, some male newts become brightly colored or grow large crests to attract females.

◁ Newts go through several stages of growth in their lives. **1** In the spring, females return to the water to mate and lay eggs. **2** These hatch into tadpoles, with feathery gills on their bodies for breathing. **3, 4** Legs and lungs begin to grow, and the gills disappear. **5** By the fall, it is an adult newt, able to crawl onto land.

▽ Newts living in water, like the great crested newt below, have moist skin. Land-living newts are called efts and have rough, dry skin. All newts return to water to breed.

△ Newts are related to salamanders. Most salamanders, like this fire salamander, live on land, and only return to the water to breed. They are poor swimmers and drown in deep water.

Find out more
Frog and Toad
Komodo dragon
and Iguana
Lizard

Octopus and Squid

The octopus is a sea creature with eight long arms, called tentacles. These can wind around objects and have suckers on them that grip. The squid is related to the octopus, but it has ten arms.

△ Octopuses can be up to 18 feet long and have an arm span of 30 feet. They live in caves on the ocean floor. When they come out, they may be attacked by sharks or moray eels—like the one seen here. If octopuses are in danger they squirt out thick black ink, which hides them while they escape. They either "walk" over the ocean floor, or they push themselves forward using a jet of water shot out of a hole in their bodies.

◁ Squid range in length from less than an inch right up to 65 feet for the largest species. Two of their ten arms are especially long and have suckers on the end.

◁ Octopuses ambush their prey, such as crabs, shellfish, and shrimp. Their tentacles draw the victim toward their powerful, birdlike beak. This is hidden at the base of the tentacles.

Find out more
Crab
Lobster and Crayfish
Shellfish
Starfish

Orangutan

The word orangutan means "man of the forest" in the Malay language, and it is true that this large ape does look a little like an old, hairy man. Orangutans live in Southeast Asia.

Fact box

• Male orangutans weigh up to 200 pounds and may grow to be 5 feet tall.
• In the wild, orangutans live about 35 years.
• When it rains, orangutans often use a large leaf as an umbrella.

▷ Baby orangutans are reared by their mothers and will stay with them until they are around five years old.

△ Orangutans have become rare partly because their forest habitat has been cut down, but also because some people think baby orangutans make good pets, and steal them from the wild. Mothers are often killed while defending their babies.

▽ Orangutans have long, strong arms. They climb slowly through the trees in the morning and evening searching for wild figs—their favorite food. At night they sleep on platforms made of branches.

Find out more
Baboon
Chimpanzee
Gorilla
Monkey

Ostrich, Emu, and Cassowary

Not all birds can fly. Although they have small wings, the world's biggest birds— ostriches, cassowaries, and emus—can only walk and run.

▽ Emus are the second tallest birds, growing to 6 feet. They live on the grasslands of Australia.

△ Ostriches lay up to eight giant eggs in a nest on the ground. The male sits on the eggs at night; the female sits during the day.

▽ Male ostriches are black and white. They are the biggest birds of all—often 8 feet tall. Females are slightly smaller and grayish-brown. They can run at 40 miles per hour.

Fact box

• Ostriches live in Africa.
• Ostrich eggs are the biggest of all bird eggs.

◁ Cassowaries live in the forests of New Guinea and Australia. They are 5 feet tall and have featherless heads with a bony helmet on the top. If attacked, they will kick and slash with their clawed feet. Their middle toe is as sharp as a dagger.

Find out more
Bird
Kiwi

Otter

Otters are mammals found near rivers and seashores around the world. Although the otter makes its home on the land, it spends much of its time in the water.

△ Female otters give birth to between one and five young in an underground burrow called a holt.

long tail: this acts like as ship's rudder to steer the otter

fur: two layers keep the otter warm and dry

eyes and nose: on top of the head so the otter can see and breathe while swimming

whiskers: help the otter feel movements in the water

▷ Otters eat fish and small animals. They are strong swimmers and well designed for hunting in the water.

feet: webbed feet for swimming fast

teeth: long, sharp teeth grip and bite prey and crack shells

claws: sharp claws help the otter dig

▽ Young otters spend lots of time playing and wrestling with each other. One of their favorite games is to slide down a snow or mud bank.

△ Sea otters are found along the northern rim of the Pacific Ocean—from California to northern Japan. They often float on their backs and sometimes carry their young on their bellies.

Find out more
Beaver
Platypus
Seal and Sea lion
Weasel

Owl

Owls are birds of prey that hunt mostly at night. They use their sensitive hearing and large eyes (which give them good night vision) to catch animals such as mice and rabbits. Owls have soft feathers that allow them to fly silently. The hooting cry of some species is easy to recognize.

△ Tawny owls were once found only in woodlands. Today, they also live in towns and cities, where they hunt mice and rats. During the day, they settle in the trees of parks and yards.

◁ The burrowing owls of North and South America live in burrows in the ground. They either dig a hole themselves or use one left by another animal, such as a gopher.

▽ Barn owls build nests in buildings, hollow trees, or old hawk's nests. The round, flat shape of the barn owl's head helps it hear its prey. Once it has caught the animal, the adult brings it to the chicks in the nest.

Fact box

• Owls can swivel their heads almost all the way around when they are listening for sounds.
• Snowy owls live in the Arctic. They mainly hunt lemmings. These owls nest on the ground.

Find out more
Bat
Bird
Eagle

Panda

The giant panda is a bear found in just a few high bamboo forests in China. There are probably no more than 1,500 giant pandas left in the wild. About 100 are kept in zoos around the world.

▽ Pandas have one or two cubs at a time. At birth, a cub weighs only 3.5 ounces. At first the mother holds it close to her chest at all times. But it grows quickly, and after ten weeks the cub starts to crawl.

△ Giant pandas usually eat only bamboo. To help them grasp the stems, they have an extra pad on their front paws that works like a thumb. Giant pandas have become rare since their forests have been cut down, and because they were once hunted for their fur.

▷ Red pandas look very much like raccoons. They live in the high forests of the Himalayas, from Nepal to China. They feed at night on roots, acorns, bamboo, and fruit.

Find out more

Bear
Mammal
Polar bear
Raccoon

Parrot

Parrots live in warm, tropical places around the world. They have strong, hooked beaks for cracking nuts and seeds. Each foot has two pairs of toes, which helps the birds perch and grip food.

▷ Macaws are brilliantly colored parrots from South America. They are large, noisy birds, and their piercing screams can often be heard in tropical rain forests.

△ Cockatoos are parrots found in Australia. This sulfur-crested cockatoo has a crest that it can raise and lower. Cockatoos are popular as pets, and often learn to copy human speech.

▷ Lovebirds are brightly-colored, small parrots from Africa and Madagascar. They get their name from the way they sit together in pairs, resting their heads against each other.

Find out more
Bird
Hummingbird
Peacock
Toucan

Peacock

The peacock is one of the world's most beautiful birds. Peacocks first lived in Asia, but because of their colorful feathers, they have been kept in parks and gardens for thousands of years. They have a loud, piercing cry and eat snails, frogs, insects, and plants.

▽ Peacocks have shiny green or blue tail feathers, tipped with a pattern like an eye. To attract females, they raise their tails and vibrate them.

▽ The female is called a peahen. Peahens have short tails, and much duller feathers than the males.

Fact box

• Peacocks have the longest tail feathers of any bird—over 5 feet.
• In 1936, a hunt started for the African Congo peacock when a single feather was discovered. The bird itself was finally found 23 years later.

▽ Pheasants are members of the same family as peacocks. Male pheasants also have long, decorative tails and brightly patterned feathers. Pheasants originally came from the Far East, but have been bred in many countries for hunting.

Find out more

Bird
Chicken and Turkey

Pelican

There is a rhyme about the pelican —"its beak can hold more than its belly can"—and this is true. The pelican's beak has a huge pouch, which holds three times as much as its stomach. It uses the pouch to scoop up fish from the water.

▷ Pelicans bring fish back for their young in their throats. The baby pelicans reach down into the throat to take the fish.

▷ The brown pelican of North and South America catches fish by diving. It flies above the sea looking for food. When it spots some fish near the surface, it dives into the water, snapping up a number of fish in one swift movement.

◁ American white pelicans use teamwork to catch fish. One group will guide the fish into shallow water by paddling their feet and moving their beaks. Once the fish are trapped, the other birds plunge their beaks in to scoop them up.

Find out more

Flamingo, Heron, and Stork

Penguin

Penguin

Penguins are seabirds that live in some of the world's coldest places. They are found on islands in the seas around Antarctica, and on the southern tips of South America, South Africa, and Australia. Penguins cannot fly, but they can swim better than any other bird.

△ Penguins swim using their small, stiff wings like flippers. Their tails and feet are used for steering. They hunt fish and krill, a type of shrimp. Waterproof feathers and layers of fat keep them warm.

◁ The Adélie penguin of the Antarctic islands lives in big, noisy colonies. When calling to attract a mate or to warn off other penguins, they throw back their heads.

△ Emperor penguins do not make nests. Instead, the male keeps the egg warm by balancing it on his feet. When the chick hatches, it huddles close to its parent's body for the first few weeks.

◁ While the emperor penguin (above) can be up to 4 feet tall, the smallest penguin is the fairy penguin, which reaches a height of just 16 inches.

Find out more
Baby animal
Ostrich, Emu, and Cassowary
Seal and Sea lion

Pig

Pigs were first tamed 9,000 years ago in China. Today most pigs are farm animals, raised for their meat and skins. Pigs eat almost anything. They are intelligent animals, and some people keep them as pets.

△ There are over 90 breeds of tame pig. They grow very quickly, and when raised on a special diet, may grow to 6.5 feet in length in just two years.

△▷ Baby pigs are called piglets. The mother pig, called a sow, usually has a litter of up to 12, and has two rows of nipples along her belly for them to drink milk from. Sometimes the weakest piglet, called a runt, is not able to feed and needs to be cared for by a human.

▽ Wild boars are fierce animals that live in forests in many countries. The piglets have striped coats that help camouflage them.

Find out more
Camouflage
Goat
Mammal
Sheep

Pigeon and Dove

Pigeons live in towns, woods, and grasslands, in all parts of the world except for very cold places. They range from the dull gray pigeons seen in cities to the brightly colored birds of the tropics. Small pigeons are called doves.

△ The rock dove was first tamed about 5,000 years ago in the Middle East. Wild rock doves still live in remote areas of Europe. The street pigeon found in towns and cities is descended from the wild rock dove.

Fact box

• The most famous extinct bird is the dodo—a big pigeon that once lived on Mauritius.
• New Guinea's crowned pigeons are turkey-sized.
• White doves are a symbol of peace. Pictures usually show them carrying an olive branch.

◁ Pigeons can find their way home over long distances. This is why homing pigeons have been used since ancient times to carry messages. In A.D. 1150 a pigeon mail service was set up by the sultan of Baghdad. Today people hold races to see whose pigeon gets home fastest. Races can be over thousands of miles.

▽ Most pigeons, like this wood pigeon, build untidy nests in trees, where the female lays one or two eggs. Pigeons in towns nest on ledges on the sides of buildings.

Find out more
Arctic tern
Bird
Conservation
Owl
Sparrow

Platypus

The platypus is a strange animal. It has a beaver's tail, a duck's bill, and webbed feet. Like a reptile, it lays eggs, but it also gives milk to its young, just as mammals do. It belongs to a small group of animals called monotremes, which have features of both mammals and reptiles.

△ The platypus is found in Australia and Tasmania. Like the otter, the platypus lives in a burrow and hunts in the water.

◁ The platypus has fur similar to an otter's. Even its flat tail is covered in fur. When it swims, the platypus paddles with its front feet and steers with its back feet and tail. It uses its sensitive, rubbery bill to find food in the muddy beds of the rivers and lakes where it lives. Platypuses eat crayfish, shrimp, worms, frogs, and small fish. They are greedy animals and eat their own weight in food every day.

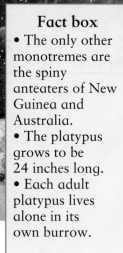

Fact box
• The only other monotremes are the spiny anteaters of New Guinea and Australia.
• The platypus grows to be 24 inches long.
• Each adult platypus lives alone in its own burrow.

▷ Before laying her eggs, the female platypus makes a nest at the end of her burrow. She lays two or three eggs, then seals the opening of the tunnel to stop predators from entering.

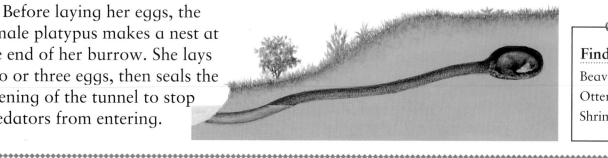

Find out more
Beaver
Otter
Shrimp and Prawn

Polar bear

Polar bears live in the frozen regions of the Arctic, where they hunt and raise their young. Their white fur makes them almost invisible in the snow. They feed mainly on seals, but also eat fish, geese, and ducks. They are the only northern bears that do not hibernate in the winter.

△ Polar bears have thick, oily coats and a layer of fat to protect them from the icy temperatures, which can drop to –32°F.

◁ Polar bears are good swimmers—they have to be to cross the moving packs of ice. They are often found swimming in the sea many miles away from an ice pack or land. Their large, furry feet make good paddles for swimming.

△ Polar bears often wait at the breathing holes of seals. When the seal comes up for air, the bear catches it, kills it, and then eats it.

Fact box
• Male polar bears weigh up to 1,800 pounds.
• Baby polar bears are born in early December in ice dens. They stay in these with their mothers until spring.

◁ Polar bears live alone and only meet when they go south to mate. They go as far as the mouth of the Amur River in Russia and the Gulf of St. Lawrence in Canada.

Find out more
Bear
Penguin
Seal and Sea lion

Porcupine

Porcupines are covered in spines called quills, and this makes them look very much like hedgehogs. However, the two are not related. Porcupines are actually rodents and they have large teeth for gnawing.

△ When a porcupine is threatened, it raises and rattles its quills. If the warning is ignored, the porcupine backs into the attacker and jabs its sharp quills into the animal's flesh.

△ Young porcupines are born with soft quills. As adults, porcupines are about 36 inches in length.

▷ Most porcupines have long quills, but the quills of the North American porcupine are short. It lives mainly in forests but also wanders into open countryside. North American porcupines climb trees to feed on leaves, berries, and bark, and often strip enough bark from a tree to kill it.

Find out more
Beaver
Hedgehog
Rat

Puffin

Puffins are small seabirds that live in cold northern parts of the Atlantic and Pacific oceans. They have big beaks that become brightly colored in the summer when they are looking for a mate. In the winter the beak is dull yellow.

△ The tufted puffin of the North Pacific is one of only three puffin species in the world. The tuft is made up of long straw-colored feathers that curve back from behind the bird's eyes.

△ Puffins live in large colonies on clifftops. They nest in long tunnels, which they either dig themselves or take over from rabbits. The females each lay a single egg here.

◁ Puffins feed mainly on sand eels, which they bring back to their nests in their beaks. Although they have a stumpy shape, puffins are fast fliers and swim underwater to catch the eels.

Find out more
Arctic tern
Bird
Duck and Goose
Gull
Penguin

Puma

Pumas are big cats found in North America and most of South America. Also known as cougars or mountain lions, they are now only found in very wild places.

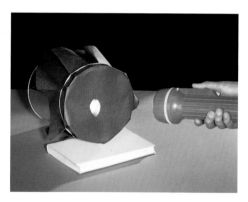

△ Pumas hunt mainly at night, so they need good hearing and eyesight to stalk their prey. Like most cats, they have a reflective layer inside their eyes that helps them see in the dark.

△ **1** To see how the puma's eyes work, cut a cat's-eye shape in black paper, then wrap the paper over the open top of a shiny can. Secure it with a rubber band.

▷ **2** In a dark room, place the can against a dark background and shine a flashlight at the "eye." You should see a cat's eye shining back at you.

Fact box
- The puma makes a noise like a domestic cat, but louder.
- The male can be as long as 10 feet, from nose to tail.
- Pumas hunt deer and small mammals.

◁ Female pumas have one to five spotted kittens, usually every other year. At two months, the kittens follow their mother on hunting trips so she can teach them how to hunt prey.

Find out more
Cat (domestic)
Cat (wild)
Cheetah
Leopard
Lion
Tiger

Rabbit and Hare

Rabbits and hares are closely related. Hares are bigger than rabbits and have longer ears and legs. Hares live aboveground, while rabbits live underground in linked-up tunnels, called warrens.

△ The black-tailed jack rabbit of the hot North American deserts is really a hare. Its very long ears help it cool down in the fierce heat of the day.

△ Rabbits were originally found in the countries around the Mediterranean Sea. Humans have now introduced them throughout the world.

▽ Rabbits are popular pets. They are friendly animals and easy to keep in outdoor hutches. They need to be fed and given fresh water every day, and their hutches must be cleaned regularly.

Fact box

• Rabbits have up to ten babies in a litter and give birth seven times a year.
• Young hares are called leverets.
• Top speed for a hare is 35 miles per hour.

Find out more

Guinea pig, Gerbil, and Hamster

Rat

Squirrel

Raccoon

The striped tail and black mask of the North American raccoon make it easy to spot. Raccoons are forest creatures, but they have learned to scavenge from humans and often make their dens near towns.

△ People's trash makes a tasty lunch for a raccoon. Raccoons will often get used to humans and can be partly tamed. However, they will always keep their wild instincts and may be fierce fighters.

Fact box

• The raccoon gets its name from a Native American word that means "scratches with hands."
• There are seven raccoon species.
• Wild raccoons live for about five years.

△ Even though they are weaned at two months, young raccoons are protected by their mother for up to a year.

▷ In the wild, raccoons eat berries, acorns, and seeds. They like to live near rivers so they can hunt for crabs, frogs, and fish. They will also rinse any dirty food in the water. When the young are old enough, they will leave their mother to live on their own.

Find out more
Bear
Beaver
Fox
Panda

Rat

Rats are rodents with sharp teeth, furry bodies, and long tails. There are over 120 types of rat, living all over the world. The brown rat and the black rat are the most common.

△ Brown rats and black rats originally came from Asia, but they are now found all over the world, wherever humans live. It is said that there is probably one rat for every person on the planet.

△ Both black and brown female rats will have between six and 22 babies in a litter. They can have up to seven litters a year.

▷ Pack rats, also called wood rats, are American rodents that live in nests made of plants. They are nocturnal and eat grasses and cereals.

Fact box

• Rats can carry about 30 diseases affecting humans.
• In the Middle Ages, one in four Europeans died from the plague—a disease spread by rats.
• Rats have been known to gnaw through electric cables!

▷ Humans see rats as pests because they spread disease and spoil human foods. They are intelligent animals and will use their sharp teeth to bite through most obstacles.

Find out more
Beaver
Guinea pig, Gerbil, and Hamster
Mouse

Rattlesnake

Rattlesnakes are found in North and South America. They are named after their spooky rattle, which warns other animals that they are very poisonous. There are about 30 species of rattlesnake.

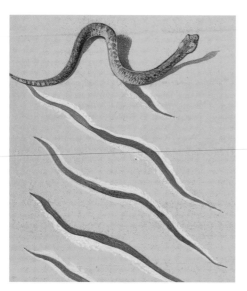

◁ The sidewinder is a rattlesnake that lives in sandy deserts in Mexico and the southwestern United States. Its unusual method of moving sideways leaves a distinctive trail.

△ Most rattlesnakes rest during the day and hunt small rodents at night. They detect prey by "tasting" the air for smells with their forked tongue. As the prey moves closer, the rattlesnake feels its body warmth with heat-sensitive pits on the sides of its face.

Fact box
• At 8 feet long, the eastern diamondback is the biggest rattlesnake.
• A rattlesnake's poison comes out of two fangs in its upper jaw.
• The bite of a rattlesnake can be deadly.

▷ Inside a rattlesnake's tail is a set of hard, loose pieces. It is these that produce the rattling noise. You can make your own rattle by threading some bottle tops onto a long nail and attaching it to a length of wood (get an adult to help you). You might scare a few people!

Find out more
Anaconda
Cobra
Communication
Defense
Reptile

Ray

Rays are fish with flat fins shaped like wings. Their eyes are on the top of the body, and the mouth underneath. Rays often lie on the ocean floor, half-buried in the sand, waiting to catch other fish and shellfish. They are found in all the world's seas, especially warm waters.

△ Manta rays measure over 22 feet across. They sometimes leap out of the water to get rid of animals living on their bodies.

Fact box
- The shock from a torpedo ray can be up to 220 volts—enough to knock down an adult human.
- The manta ray is often called the devilfish because of its horns.
- The manta ray uses its horns to guide tiny sea animals like plankton into its mouth.

△ Torpedo rays are also called electric rays, because they give their prey an electric shock to stun it. The electricity is made in muscles in the ray's head.

▷ The spines on a stingray's tail can give a painful sting.

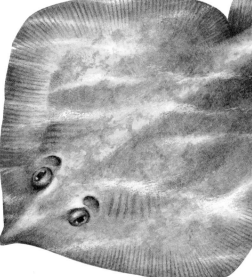

Find out more
Eel
Flatfish
Jellyfish
Shark

Reindeer

Reindeer are found in the Arctic regions of Asia, Europe, and North America. They live on the tundra (plains) and in forests. The reindeer is closely related to the caribou of North America.

▽ Like all other deer, reindeer lose their antlers in the spring, then grow a new set that reaches full size in the fall. Reindeer are the only deer where the females have antlers as well as males.

▽ People first tamed the reindeer over 3,000 years ago, and they have been used as transportation and for their meat and fur ever since. Humans have never managed to tame the caribou.

△ Reindeer feed on grass, lichens, and twigs. In the winter they use their large hooves to shovel the snow away to dig for food. In the winter their thick coats are gray; in the summer they are brown.

◁ Reindeer and caribou migrate over long distances. They move south in the fall and north in the spring. Young or weak animals are often preyed on by hungry wolves.

Find out more
Deer
Elk
Mammal
Migration

Reproduction

From the huge whale to the tiny ant, all animals must reproduce (make babies), so that their species can survive. There are many different ways of doing this.

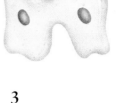

△ The amoeba is a microscopic animal made of just one cell. Its way of reproducing is very simple —it splits in half. The new cells will reproduce in the same way.

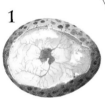

▽ **1** When two birds mate, the male fertilizes an egg inside the female. Soon a baby chick starts to grow. **2** As it grows, the chick feeds off the white and then the yolk of the egg. **3, 4** When it is ready to hatch, the chick pecks at the eggshell and breaks out.

△ The babies of almost all mammals grow inside their mothers and are born live. They must be fed and protected until they can take care of themselves.

◁ You can help birds bring up their young by putting up a nesting box on a tree or a building. Make sure it is between 6 and 16 feet above the ground. Keep a record of the changes you see.

▷ While most reproduction needs a male and a female, earthworms are both male and female at once. The thick saddle in the middle of the body produces eggs that can be fertilized by any other worm.

saddle

Find out more
Bird
Baby animal
Mammal
Microscopic animal

Reptile

Reptiles are animals with scaly skin. Some species live on land, others live in water. There are many different kinds of reptile, including turtles, snakes, and crocodiles. They live in the warmer parts of the world.

△ Although some snakes are dangerous to humans, many are harmless and can be kept as pets. Their skin feels dry and not slimy, as some people expect.

△ To make your own reptile collage, draw the shape of a lizard on a piece of cardboard. Using different colored lentils or beans, glue the "scales" on in stripes.

▷ Reptiles cannot control their own body temperature. To get warm, these lizards must sit in the sun. To cool down, they have to move to the shade.

▽ Some reptiles have tongues that act like noses. Instead of sniffing the air to pick up a scent, they stick out their tongues and "taste" it. This helps them find their prey.

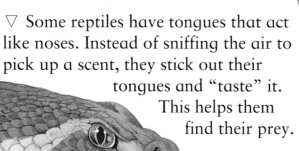

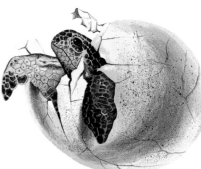

△ Most reptiles lay eggs. While the shells of turtle and crocodile eggs are hard, snake and lizard eggs are soft and leathery.

Find out more

Alligator and Crocodile

Komodo dragon and Iguana

Lizard

Rattlesnake

Turtle and Tortoise

Rhinoceros

Rhinoceroses (or rhinos) are large, heavy animals that live on open grassland in Asia and Africa. They are protected from predators by tough, armored skin and sharp horns. Although rhino horn is very hard, it is actually made of a material similar to hair.

△ Rhinos weigh up to 5.5 tons and can charge at 30 miles per hour.

▽ Rhinos have poor eyesight, but a very good sense of smell. Females with young calves are likely to charge if they feel threatened by an unfamiliar sound or scent, and males are often bad-tempered. But rhinos will let birds called oxpeckers ride on their backs and feed on insects living on the rhino's skin.

Indian rhino   African white rhino   African black rhino

△ African rhinos have two horns; Asian rhinos have one. Indian rhinos have a long upper lip for eating reeds and grass. The white rhino, which is actually gray, has a wide upper lip for grazing. The black rhino uses its pointed upper lip to eat leaves.

Find out more
Elephant
Hippopotamus
Horse
Pig

Salmon and Trout

Salmon and some kinds of trout are found in the cold northern parts of the Atlantic and Pacific oceans. Most types of trout, however, live in fresh water. Large salmon can weigh over 65 pounds, while the largest trout weigh over 30 pounds.

△ There are many different types of trout. The brightly colored rainbow trout (above) is one of the most common. It was introduced to Europe from North America and people often catch it for sport.

▽ Before they breed, salmon migrate thousands of miles from their homes in the sea, back to the rivers where they were born. They battle upstream against strong currents, clearing obstacles such as waterfalls by leaping up to 11 feet high.

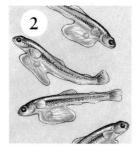

▽ **3** After a year the young salmon develop red stripes on their sides. **4** By the time they are 6 inches long, the salmon are silver colored. They are now ready to journey down the river to the sea, where they will grow into adults and repeat the cycle.

△ **1** The female salmon makes a small hole in the gravel on the riverbed and lays her eggs. The male then fertilizes them. **2** At birth, young salmon have a pouch on their sides that contains food.

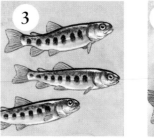

Find out more
Fish
Migration
Reproduction
Swordfish

Scorpion

Scorpions are part of the same group of animals as spiders—the arachnids. They have eight legs, two powerful claws, and a stinging tail. Scorpions hide by day and only come out at night.

stinging tail

claw

▷ Scorpions catch their prey in their claws and use the sting in their tail to kill it. The sting is also used in defense against predators like mongooses. Most scorpion stings are similar to those of a wasp, but some are strong enough to kill humans.

▽ Female scorpions keep their eggs inside their bodies until they are ready to hatch. When the young scorpions are born, they climb onto their mother's back.

△ Male scorpions may fight over a mate, wrestling with their claws and trying to sting each other. Before mating, the male and female also grapple in a complicated dance.

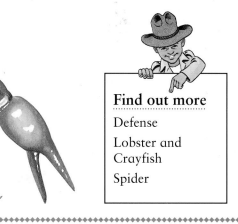

Find out more
Defense
Lobster and Crayfish
Spider

Seabird

Some birds spend their whole lives near the sea, eating fish and nesting on cliffs or beaches. These birds are well adapted to life near the ocean: they usually have webbed feet for swimming, a sharp bill for catching fish, and waterproof feathers.

◁ **1** Seabirds need waterproof feathers so they don't get soggy and sink. Squirt water at a seabird feather and you will see how the natural oils on the feather repel the water.

△ Gannets are large, white seabirds with black-tipped wings. They fly above the surface of the water until they spot a school of fish. Then they dive deep into the ocean.

▷ **2** Take an even closer look at the feather with a magnifying glass. Can you see how the barbs link together? This flat surface is called the vane.

◁ Some seabirds, such as gulls and skuas, always stay near the shore. Others, like albatrosses and petrels, roam far out to sea. But all seabirds must return to land to nest. Guillemot eggs (left) have pointed ends, so they will roll in a circle instead of falling off the cliff.

Find out more
Albatross
Bird
Fish
Gull
Pelican
Penguin
Puffin

Sea cow

The dugong and the manatee are sea cows. They are mammals that live in warm tropical seas, feeding on sea grass and water plants. The dugong is found in the Indian and Pacific oceans. The manatee lives in the tropical waters of the Americas, the West Indies, and Africa.

△ The dugong has a V-shaped tail. Adults grow to be 11 feet long. Unlike the manatee, male dugongs grow two tusklike teeth.

Fact box
- Female sea cows give birth to one baby at a time.
- Sea cows nurse their babies on nipples on their chest. They can hold the baby to a nipple with a flipper.
- Amazonian manatees gather in groups of 500.

▽ Manatees have round tails, shaped like paddles. They swim slowly and have bad eyesight.

△ Sea cows may live alone or in small groups. They seem to be affectionate animals— manatees often greet each other by touching noses, which looks as if they are kissing.

△ In the 1700s, sailors used to kill manatees for food. Manatees are now a protected species, but they are sometimes injured by boat propellers while swimming in shallow water.

Find out more
Dolphin
Seal and Sea lion
Walrus
Whale

Seahorse

Seahorses are fish that live in warm seas. Because they swim upright and are covered by bony armor, they do not look like fish. However, they are related to the stickleback.

▷ When seahorses mate, the male and female meet belly to belly and the female lays her eggs in a pouch on the male. Five weeks later, up to 200 young hatch from his body, looking just like tiny adults.

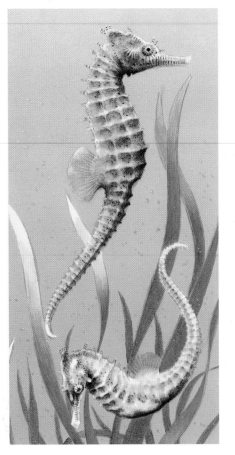

△ Seahorses spend much of their lives anchored by their tails to seaweed. They feed on shrimp and plankton, which they suck into their long mouths.

◁ The sea dragon is a type of seahorse found around the coasts of Australia. It is 5 feet long and is camouflaged by leafy-looking growths all over its body.

Find out more
Camouflage
Coral reef
Fish
Reproduction

Seal and Sea lion

Seals and sea lions are good swimmers and divers. They are mammals, so they have to come up to breathe, but they can stay underwater for up to 30 minutes. They feed on fish and penguins.

▽ While sea lions can walk on their flippers, seals cannot. Male sea lions have thick fur on their necks that looks like the mane of a lion.

▽ Seals catch their prey underwater, then they come to the surface to eat it.

◁ Female seals and sea lions feed their babies on milk that is extremely nourishing. The milk is full of fat and helps the babies grow quickly.

▽ Male elephant seals are the largest seals in the world. They get their name from their floppy noses, which look like trunks.

Fact box
• The Baikal seal of Russia is the only freshwater seal in the world.
• Sea lion colonies sometimes have hundreds of thousands of sea lions in them.
• Monk seals are one of the few species to live in tropical water, such as the Caribbean Sea.

Find out more
Dolphin
Killer whale
Penguin
Whale

Shark

Sharks are the most fearsome predators in the ocean. They are excellent hunters and find their prey either by its smell, or by tracking the tiny electrical currents that the prey's body gives out.

great white shark

△ The world's most dangerous shark is the great white. It can grow to be 40 feet long, and has a huge mouth full of sharp, pointed teeth. Great whites are found in warm waters all over the world. They sometimes attack bathers and surfers, but seals and sea lions are their favorite prey.

hammerhead shark

◁ The hammerhead shark uses its huge head to steer itself. Sharks are a kind of fish, but instead of fish scales they have rough skin, and instead of bone their skeleton is made of rubbery cartilage.

◁ At over 49 feet long, the whale shark is the largest of all fish. It eats some of the smallest creatures in the sea—plankton.

Find out more
Dolphin
Ray
Killer whale
Seal and Sea lion

Sheep

Sheep were first tamed in the Middle East over 7,000 years ago. They are kept all over the world for their wool, meat, and skins. Female sheep are called ewes, males are called rams, and the young are called lambs.

Hampshire down

Southdown

Romney

Scottish black face

△ Farm sheep can have two or three lambs at a time. Some newborn lambs are very weak and may need to be hand-reared. Wild sheep only give birth to one lamb.

◁ Today there are about 700 million sheep on farms all over the world. There are more than 800 breeds, each suited to different climates and producing different types of wool.

▷ Wild sheep have hairy coats to protect them from the cold mountain climate. In the winter, they grow a thick undercoat of fine wool called fleece, which falls out (molts) in the spring. Farm sheep are sheared before they molt, giving us wool.

Find out more
Cow and Bull
Goat
Mammal
Pig

Shellfish

Shellfish are water creatures whose soft bodies are protected by hard shells. Like slugs, snails, and octopuses, they are mollusks. They are found in fresh water and salt water all over the world.

△ When shellfish die, all that remains is the shell. If you go to the beach, collect as many different shells as you can. Later, you can display them on a board with their names underneath them.

Fact box

- Some shellfish have just one shell, others have a pair.
- Shells are made of minerals. These make the shells very hard.
- Shellfish have existed on Earth for 600 million years.

◁ Most shellfish feed by filtering tiny food particles from the water. Some shellfish stay on the same rock all their lives. They anchor themselves with a single sucker foot, or by threads.

▽ Mussels have two matching shells that clamp shut when they are in danger. They hold on to rocks using threads that are so strong they can resist huge storm waves.

lambis shell   **top shell**

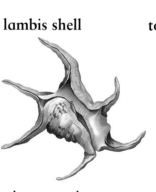   

tiger cowrie

Find out more

Crab

Octopus and Squid

Shrimp and Prawn

Shrimp and prawns live in oceans, rivers, and lakes almost everywhere. They are related to lobsters but are smaller and are better swimmers. Prawns are slightly bigger than shrimp.

△ The pistol shrimp, which grows to about an inch and a half long, has very large claws. It snaps them together to stun its prey.

▽ **1** Make an underwater viewer to look at shrimp and prawns in rock pools. Get an adult to cut the bottom off a clear plastic bottle. Stretch plastic wrap over the cut end and secure with a rubber band.

▽ **2** You will need to keep still— these animals are easily frightened.

Norway lobster

ghost shrimp

female common prawn

male common prawn

common shrimp

◁ Shrimp and prawns often search for food on the seabed. They eat small plants and animals. They swim by flicking their fanlike tails.

Find out more
Crab
Lobster
and Crayfish
Shellfish

Skunk

Skunks live in woods and grassland in North and South America. They have long, furry tails and black and white fur. They are known for the foul smell they give off in defense.

△ Skunks are about the size of domestic cats, and weigh up to 7 pounds. They rest in their burrows by day, and come out at night to find plants, birds' eggs, insects, and small mammals to eat.

△ Skunks have around three babies in the spring. The young are born blind and do not leave the burrow for six weeks. When full-grown, they leave to find their own home.

▽ The skunk has a special way of dealing with a predator such as a lynx. First it thumps its paws on the ground. Then it turns around, flinging up its rear legs to expose its bottom.

Fact box
• The most common skunk in North America is the striped skunk.
• The other two types are the hognosed skunk and the spotted skunk.
• Skunks can spray an attacker from a distance of 13 feet. The smell lasts for days.

▷ If the attacker does not heed the warning, the skunk lowers its legs and squirts a jet of liquid from glands near the tail. The smell is so awful that few predators return for more.

Find out more
Badger
Otter
Weasel

Sloth

Someone who is lazy or slow might be described as being slothful. Looking at the sloth, it is easy to see why. The sloth spends its life hanging in the trees by its hooked claws, and it hardly ever moves at all.

Fact box
- Sloths are found in the rain forests of South America.
- Once every two to three weeks, they climb down to the ground to go to the bathroom.
- Sloths can fall asleep in their hanging position.

▽ The female gives birth to one young, which she carries on her stomach for about five weeks after its birth. The baby sloth stays on by clinging to its mother's fur.

△ Sloths wake at night to feed on leaves and fruit. The hair on their coats hangs down from the belly to the back so the rainwater can flow off easily. Some species have algae growing in their coats. This gives them a greenish color that camouflages them in the trees.

△ Although sloths move slowly on land, they can swim well. They are not afraid to cross large rivers and swamps to find food and new trees to live in.

Find out more
Camouflage
Mammal
Monkey

Slug and Snail

Slugs and snails are found all over the world, both on land and in water. They have feelers on their heads, soft bodies, and a single muscular foot that is also their stomach. Snails have shells, but slugs do not.

◁ Watch how slugs and snails move by placing them on a piece of clear glass or plastic. You will see that they ooze a trail of slime to ease their way along.

△ Garden slugs and snails feed mainly on rotting plants. But sometimes they eat growing plants, so they can be bad for gardens. Their mouths are full of tiny teeth.

▽ Snails are known for moving slowly, but a snail race can still be very exciting. On a board, make three lanes with string held in place by tacks. Chalk a line at the start and at the finish, then start them off. The first one past the finish line is the winner.

Fact box

• Land species have lungs to breathe; water species have gills.
• The giant land snail can be 12 inches long.
• Tropical cone snails feed on fish. First they paralyze them by injecting nerve poison from a tooth on the end of their tongue.

Find out more
Centipede
Defense
Fish
Habitat
Shellfish
Worm

Sparrow

Sparrows are small birds that are found all over the world. Seeds are their main food, but they feed insects to their young. There are around 50 species in North and South America alone.

female house sparrow

male house sparrow

△ House sparrows live mostly in towns and cities in small flocks near houses. They have a twittering song and will often fight among themselves.

△ 1 Make a special cake for the sparrows that live near you. Warm some fat on a radiator. Then mix it with some seeds, breadcrumbs, oats, and fruit in a large bowl. Press the mix into molds such as yogurt pots.

▽ 2 Once it sets, tip the mixture out onto a bird table or window ledge.

▷ The song sparrow of North America has a very tuneful song. Young song sparrows learn their songs in the fall and sing them the following spring.

Find out more
Bird
Food
Habitat
Pigeon
Swift and Swallow

Spider

Spiders belong to the class of animals called arachnids. They feed mainly on insects. Most spiders have large, hairy, round abdomens (rear body parts) and eight legs. All spiders make silk, and many spin webs.

◁ The female black widow spider is one of the few spiders with venom (poison) harmful to humans. Most people bitten by it do recover fully.

Fact box

• The goliath bird-eating spider is the biggest spider in the world. It is large enough to cover a dinner plate.
• Tropical orb-web spiders build some of the largest webs—nearly 7 feet across.

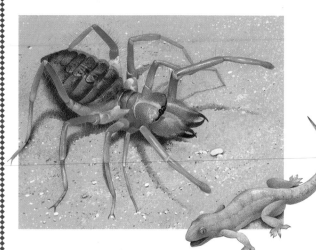

△ Camel spiders live in deserts in Africa and Asia. They do not spin webs, but pounce on their prey and crush them in their strong jaws. They feed on scorpions, birds, and small lizards.

▷ Many spiders spin webs of sticky silk to catch their prey. Silk is very strong and it also stretches. Here a garden spider wraps a fly in its silk, then stuns it with venom from its fangs.

◁ Spiders live in many places, from hot deserts to mountains and lakes. Some spiders that live near water eat small fish.

Find out more
Fly
Insect
Scorpion

Squirrel

Most squirrels have big, bushy tails and live in trees. They are active during the day, running from branch to branch in search of nuts, fruit, and seeds.

▷ The red squirrel, like the one seen here, is smaller than its gray cousin. In Britain, red squirrels are being forced from their woodland homes by the more aggressive gray squirrels, which were imported from North America about 100 years ago.

▽ The prairie dog is a burrowing squirrel that lives on North American grasslands. Their large underground burrows, called towns, contain up to 1,000 prairie dogs.

◁ Squirrels love seeds like acorns, which they gnaw with their sharp front teeth. In the fall, they sometimes bury a supply in the ground to last them through the winter.

Find out more
Habitat
Mammal
Mouse
Rat
Reproduction

Starfish

Starfish are found on ocean floors worldwide, especially in the warm waters of the Indian and Pacific oceans. Though starfish are star-shaped, they are not fish. They have no head and no brain; all they have is five or more arms, a central body, and a mouth.

1

2

3

4

◁ A starfish has hundreds of strong suckers called tube feet. If it is turned upside down it uses these tube feet to turn over again. **1** It curls the tips of its arms around to grip the rocks with its suckers. **2** When it has a hold, it pulls itself over slowly. **3, 4** It flops down the right way up, and moves off.

△ There are 1,500 species of starfish in the world's oceans. Many are brightly colored.

▷ Some kinds of starfish have lots of legs, like this sunstar. If a starfish loses a leg, it can easily grow another.

▽ Starfish eat shellfish. To eat a mussel, the starfish opens the shell with its powerful suckers, then pushes its stomach out of its mouth and onto the body of the shellfish.

Fact box

• The crown-of-thorns starfish feeds on coral, and this can badly damage the reef.
• Starfish sense changes in light with the light-sensitive spots on the ends of their arms.
• Some starfish lay up to a million eggs in a year.

Find out more

Coral reef

Octopus and Squid

Shellfish

Shrimp and Prawn

Swan

The swan is one of the world's largest water birds, with a wingspan of up to 10 feet. It has webbed feet for swimming and a wide beak for eating underwater plants. Swans guard their eggs closely and will attack humans if they feel threatened.

trumpeter swan

△ Swans in the Northern Hemisphere are white. Most are named after their calls, such as the trumpeter, whistling, and whooper swans. The whistling swan migrates from the Canadian Arctic to spend the winter in the southern United States.

▽ Southern swans include the Australian black swan and the South American black-necked swan.

Fact box

• Swans live for 20 years or more.
• Swans swallow stones to help their digestion. But many have accidentally eaten fishermen's lead weights and been poisoned by them.
• Swans build a big nest that can float on the water.

△ Swans mate when they are five years old, and the pairs remain loyal for life. Young swans, called cygnets, have fluffy gray feathers and short necks that make them look more like scruffy ducks. Their long necks and white plumage grow when they are a year old.

Australian black swan

Find out more
Bird
Duck and Goose
Migration
Pelican

Swift and Swallow

Swifts and swallows are among the fastest and most agile of fliers. They may fly nonstop for hours on end. Swifts have longer wings and fly higher than swallows. They hardly ever touch the ground. Swallows fly lower and sometimes rest on wires, roofs, and trees.

△ Swifts are well adapted to constant flight. In fact, a swift is stranded if it lands on the ground, because its wings are too long and its legs are too short for it to take off.

▽ Swallows and swifts, like this Alpine swift, catch insects in flight at high speed. Bristles around their beaks guide the prey into their large mouths.

△ A pair of swallows works together to build a mud nest, often under the roofs of houses. They bring insects to their hungry young.

Fact box
• Although the swift and the swallow look alike, they are not related.
• Swifts can fly at 43 mph.
• Tree swallows nest in holes in hollow trees.
• Swifts and swallows are found in all parts of the world.

▷ In the late summer, after they have raised their young, swallows migrate south to escape the cold winters and to search for food. Some birds that breed in Europe fly all the way to southern Africa. They return in the summer each year to the same nest sites.

Europe

Africa

Find out more
Arctic tern
Bird
Migration
Reproduction

Swordfish

The swordfish gets its name from its long upper jaw, which is shaped like a sword. It is related to the marlin and the sailfish. They are all found in the warm waters of the Atlantic, Indian, and Pacific oceans. Powerful and fast, these hunters feed on small fish.

▽ Sailfish can reach around 200 pounds in weight and 10 feet in length. To gain speed when hunting schools of fish, they sometimes leap out of the water.

Fact box

• Swordfish and marlin can reach 62 mph when chasing prey. This makes them two of the fastest fish in the sea.
• The biggest marlin can weigh up to 1,500 pounds.

△ The swordfish has a strong tail and a streamlined body—ideal for fast swimming. It uses its long bill to herd and catch smaller fish to eat.

◁ Marlin have shorter bills than swordfish, and are strong and fearless. They are often hunted for sport and have been known to ram fishing boats.

Find out more
Deep-sea fish
Fish
Shark
Whale

Tarantula

Tarantulas are large, hairy spiders found in the warmer parts of North and South America. Unlike many other spiders, most tarantulas do not spin webs. Instead, they catch their prey by ambushing it.

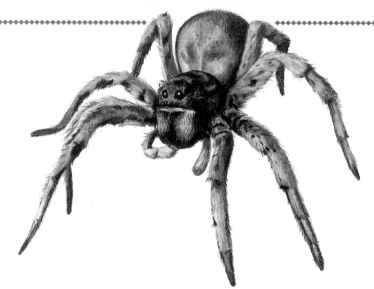

△ Like many spiders, tarantulas have venom for paralyzing or killing their prey. They only bite humans in self-defense, and although their bite is painful, the venom is not deadly.

Fact box

• One tarantula lived to be 30 years old.
• Tarantulas can have bodies that are 2 inches long.
• The legs of a tarantula can spread across 5 inches—nearly as wide as a man's palm.

◁ Many species of tarantula make burrows in the ground. They feed mostly at night and like to eat insects as well as frogs, toads, and mice. They can run quickly over short distances.

▷ If a tarantula does not feel threatened, it can be safe to handle—that is if you want to hold a giant hairy spider!

◁ Tarantulas are sometimes kept as pets and are very calm in quiet surroundings. They become especially relaxed after they have eaten.

Find out more
Insect
Mouse
Scorpion
Spider

Tiger

Tigers are the biggest of all cats. They live in the grasslands and forests of Asia, where their striped coat gives them good camouflage when they hunt.

△ Female tigers give birth to between one and three cubs. The cubs stay with their mother for over a year.

△ A tiger slowly stalks its prey, a deer, through the long grass. When it is close enough, it makes a sudden dash, leaps onto the deer's back, and knocks it down. A quick bite to the neck kills the deer.

◁ Tigers are hunted for their beautiful coats, and for their bones and body parts, which are used in traditional Chinese medicine. Because of this, tigers are nearly extinct.

Find out more
Cat (wild)
Cheetah
Leopard
Lion

Toucan

Toucans live in the tropical forests of the Americas. Their colorful beaks are thought to frighten off other birds. Although the beak is almost as big as the bird's body, it is very light. Toucans also have long tails to help them balance.

▽ Toucans gather in the treetops to roost and to feed on fruit. In order to swallow, they have to juggle their food in their beaks, then toss back their heads and catch it.

Fact box

• There are almost 40 species of toucan. The largest are up to 24 inches long.
• The larger toucans sometimes eat eggs, small birds, frogs, and lizards.
• Toucans are some of the noisiest birds in the forest. Their calls include loud croaks, barks, and hoots.

▷ Bristles at the end of the toucan's long tongue act like a brush, helping it hold on to its food.

◁ The hornbills of Africa, Asia, and some Pacific islands also have large beaks. They get their name from the hornlike structure on top of their beaks, which are strong enough to crush small reptiles.

Find out more
Bird
Flamingo, Heron, and Stork
Hummingbird

Turtle and Tortoise

Turtles and tortoises are reptiles that live in warm climates. Turtles are found in water; tortoises are slow land animals. The soft bodies of both animals are protected by a heavy shell.

Fact box
• The marine green turtle can swim 300 miles in only ten days.
• Terrapin is the name given to some freshwater turtles.
• The huge marine leatherback turtle can be 9 feet long.

△ Many turtles spend nearly all their lives in the sea. Their legs are shaped like paddles, which help them swim. Only females ever come onto land. They do this to lay eggs—on the same beach as they were born.

◁ Tortoises are found in Africa, Asia, Europe, and North and South America. They grow slowly and can live to be over 150 years old.

◁ 1 The female turtle crawls out of the sea to lay her eggs. 2 She buries them in a hole, then returns to the water. The sun's heat keeps them warm until they are ready to hatch.

▷ 3 Left on their own, the tiny babies must break free of their eggs and dig their way out of the hole. 4 They must hurry to the sea before they are eaten by other animals.

Find out more
Chameleon
Lizard
Reptile
Reproduction

Vulture

Vultures are large, strange-looking birds with wide wingspans. They are found worldwide—on mountains and plains, and in forests. They feed on rotting meat.

◁ Many species of vulture, like the king vulture (left), have no head or neck feathers. This keeps them clean when feeding. The king vulture's brightly colored skin flaps are used in mating displays.

△ Many vulture species have incredible eyesight. They fly high in the air, looking for predators' kills.

▽ Vultures do a vital job because they clean up the carcasses left behind by predators. Once they spot a carcass, they glide down to feed. Some vultures have adapted to living in towns, and scavenge on garbage dumps.

△ Vultures, like this white-backed vulture, often sit in the trees around a lion or hyena kill, waiting until the larger animals have had their fill.

Eurasian griffin

Ruppell's griffin

African white-backed vulture

lappet-faced vulture

Find out more
Bird
Eagle
Owl

Walrus

Walruses are sea mammals that live along the edges of the ice in the cold Arctic waters of the Atlantic and Pacific oceans. Both males and females have two long, white, ivory tusks. Their wrinkled skin covers a thick layer of blubber (fat) that helps keep them warm.

△ Walruses like to sun themselves for a while before plunging back into the freezing Arctic waters. They may form large colonies on beaches. In the past, large numbers of walruses were killed for meat, for oil, and for their tusks. Today they are a protected species and are growing in number.

△ Like sea lions, walruses walk on land by turning their flippers under their body and can support themselves on all four limbs.

▷ Walrus tusks are up to 16 inches long. Males use their tusks to defend themselves and to fight over females. Both sexes also use their tusks to haul themselves onto the ice and to dig for their food—shellfish, which they find by using their bristly whiskers.

Find out more
Dolphin
Sea cow
Seal and Sea lion
Whale

Weasel

Stoats, polecats, ferrets, and minks are all members of the weasel family. These small, fierce hunters with long, slim bodies and short legs are found on every continent except Australasia.

molting stoat

stoat in winter

stoat in summer

ferret

▷ Polecats live in woods and farmland in Europe, Asia, and North America. They were tamed over 2,000 years ago, and their relatives, ferrets, may be kept as pets.

Steppe polecat

polecat

△ Stoats and weasels hunt mice, rats, and other rodents for food. Weasels are so slim that they can get right down into the burrows of their prey. They also eat fish and birds' eggs. Stoats are larger. In the far North, they turn white in winter and are called ermines.

▽ Mink are shorter and fatter than polecats. They are often bred on farms for their thick fur and are now found in a variety of colors.

American minks

Fact box
• Weasels will kill animals much bigger than themselves.
• The wolverine is the biggest of the weasel family. It grows up to 45 inches long.
• All members of the weasel family have large anal glands that they use to mark their home territory.

Find out more
Badger
Otter
Raccoon
Skunk

Whale

Whales are the biggest creatures that have ever lived on Earth —even bigger than dinosaurs. Like dolphins, whales are mammals and breathe through blowholes on their backs. They are found in all the oceans of the world.

△ The blue whale is the largest animal on Earth. It measures up to 100 feet long and weighs over 100 tons—as much as 15 elephants.

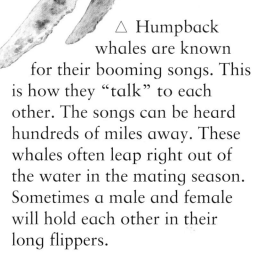

△ Humpback whales are known for their booming songs. This is how they "talk" to each other. The songs can be heard hundreds of miles away. These whales often leap right out of the water in the mating season. Sometimes a male and female will hold each other in their long flippers.

Fact box
• Blue whale babies are over 20 feet long when they are born.
• Sperm whales can hold their breath for about 70 minutes.
• Many whales feed on one of the smallest creatures in the sea—the shrimplike krill.

◁ Sperm whales eat giant squid. They hunt them deep under the sea—over 1,500 feet down. The whale's skin has scars on it from the battles between these huge animals.

Find out more
Dolphin
Killer whale
Octopus and
Squid

Wolf

Wolves are the largest of the wild dogs. They are natural hunters that work in packs when tracking their prey. Because of their sharp fangs and spooky howl, many people are afraid of wolves and believe that they will attack humans. But we are rarely on the menu.

△ Wolves have long been hunted by humans. They are now found only in the remote northern areas of Asia, Europe, and North America.

◁ Wolves live in family groups headed by one or two lead wolves. Young wolves are energetic animals and spend much of their time play-fighting. When they are older, they are taught to hunt by their parents.

▽ The wolf pack will chase its prey until it is exhausted and easier to capture. They hunt various animals, from small rodents to big caribou (reindeer) and musk oxen.

Find out more

Dog (wild)
Fox
Mammal
Reindeer

Worm

Worms are soft-bodied animals
with no backbone or legs.
Some live in water, some in
soil (like the earthworm),
and some even live inside
other animals.

◁ Hold an earthworm
in your hand, and you
will see the segments
of its body. It squeezes
and stretches these to
move along.

▽ Earthworms dig their way
through soil by eating it. Soil goes in
the front end of the worm and comes
out the back end. Piles of softened
soil are called worm casts.

△ Try making your own worm farm.
Put alternate layers of soil and sand
into a large glass jar. Place some
worms on the top, with leaves for them
to eat, then cover the jar with mesh
secured with a rubber band. Wrap
black paper around the jar. After a
couple of days, take off the paper and
see what the worms have done to the
layers and leaves. Release the worms
back into the wild after about a week.

worm cast

insect grub

coiled worm

Find out more
Centipede
Coral reef
Microscopic
animal
Reproduction
Slug and Snail

Yak

Yaks are huge, shaggy oxen found on the high plains and mountains of Tibet. Their thick coats keep them warm in the bitter mountain winters. Some are wild, but most are kept as domestic animals.

△ The coats of domestic yaks (above) come in a range of colors from white to black. Wild yaks have long, silky black or brown coats and are bigger than domestic yaks.

▽ The yak was tamed over 2,000 years ago and gives the Tibetan people milk, meat, leather, wool, and transportation. Yaks are surefooted in rocky places and can survive in the harshest conditions.

◁Wild yaks are nearly 6.5 feet high at the shoulder. The females and young live together in herds. The males prefer to live in smaller groups.

Find out more

Bison and Musk ox
Buffalo

Zebra

Closely related to horses, zebras are grazing mammals that live on the grasslands of Africa, south of the Sahara desert. Their striped coats make it hard for other animals to spot them. Even if they are seen, zebras can run faster than most of their predators.

△ Zebras live in family groups with one stallion (male), several mares (females), and their foals (young). If threatened by a lion, the mares lead the foals to safety, while the stallion kicks out with his powerful back legs.

△ Zebra stripes are like human fingerprints—no two patterns are the same. Grevy's zebra (above) has much finer stripes than the other species.

Fact box

• Zebras are smaller than horses: 7 feet long and 4 feet tall.
• Young females leave the family at two years old. They must then search for a new family to join.
• Males leave the family at four years old.

△ When there is plenty of grass to eat and water to drink, several zebra families may join together to form a large herd. If food becomes scarce, the herd may migrate long distances to find new grasslands, sometimes crossing wide rivers.

Find out more
Antelope
Donkey
Giraffe
Horse

Glossary

A **glossary** is a list of useful words. Some of the words used in this book may be new to you. You can find out more about them here.

ambush to lie in hiding, waiting to attack.

antennae a pair of thin, movable feelers on the heads of insects.

carnivore an animal that eats the meat of other animals.

carrion the rotting remains of a dead animal, often left over after a predator has finished with its kill.

cell the basic unit of life. All living things are made up of cells.

domestic animal an animal that is tame and is used to living near people.

endangered species if a species is at risk of dying out, it is described as being endangered.

environment the surroundings or the place where an animal lives.

extinct an animal species that has died out is extinct.

herbivore an animal that eats plants only.

invertebrate an animal without a backbone.

kill a dead animal that has been killed by another.

mate a male and female animal mate, or pair up, to reproduce.

mature full-grown or adult. An immature animal is a young animal.

nocturnal a nocturnal animal sleeps or rests during the day and comes out at night.

omnivore an animal that eats both plants and meat.

plankton tiny plants and animals that float in oceans, rivers, and lakes.

predator an animal that kills and eats other animals for food.

prehensile gripping. Many monkeys have prehensile tails to help them climb among the trees.

prey an animal that is hunted or killed by another animal for food.

rodent a group of small mammals, including rats and squirrels, with sharp front teeth for gnawing.

savanna warm, dry grassland with just a few small trees.

scavenge animals that scavenge do not hunt and kill their own meat, but feed on the remains of a dead animal left behind by predators.

species a particular kind of animal. The animals in a species all look alike and behave in a similar way. Animals can only breed with members of their own species. There are about a million animal species on the Earth.

tropics the warm lands that lie on either side of the Earth's equator. Tropical forests are hot and wet.

tundra the flat, treeless land in the Arctic. The ground is so cold here that only a few small plants can grow.

vertebrate an animal with a backbone.

young the offspring, or babies, of adult animals.

Index

This index helps you find subjects in the book. It is in alphabetical order. Main entries are in **dark,** or **bold,** type

O

octopus 46, 98, 132
omnivore 18, 90
opossum **82**
orangutan **99**
ostrich **100**
otter **101**, 110
owl 38, 62, **102**

P

panda **103**
panther 85
parrot **104**
peacock **105**
pelican **106**
penguin 17, **107**, 129
phytoplankton 62
pig 73, 83, 85, **108**
pigeon **109**
plankton 119, 128, 130
platypus 90, **110**
poison (venom) 37, 46, 64,
    78, 87, 118, 136,
    138, 144
polar bear 20, **111**
pond 9, 21
pony 74
porcupine **112**
prawn **133**
primate 84, 90, 95
puffin **113**
puma 56, 62, **114**

R

rabbit 31, 102, 113, **115**
raccoon 103, **116**
rat 102, **117**, 150
rattlesnake **118**
ray **119**
reindeer **120**, 152
reproduction 22, 27, **121**
reptile 8, 87, 110, **122**,
    146, 147
rhinoceros 76, **123**
rodent 21, 69, 96,
    112, 117, 118, 139, 150, 152

S

salmon 20, **124**
scavenger 63, 70, 83, 116, 148
scorpion 42, **125**, 138
seabird 7, 14, 70, 107, 113, **126**
sea cow **127**
seahorse **128**
seal 62, 80, 111, **129**, 130
sea lion **129**, 130
shark 98, **130**
sheep **131**
shell 32, 42, 46, 89, 101,
    122, 132, 136, 147
shellfish 60, 98, 119, **132**, 140, 149
shrimp 59, 98, 110, 128, **133**
skin 9, 10, 41, 64, 66, 87, 92,
    97, 108, 122, 123, 130,
    131, 149
skunk 18, **134**
sloth 53, **135**
slug 71, 132, **136**
smell (scent) 38, 48, 66, 83,
    118, 122, 123, 130, 134, 150
smell (sense of) 20, 38, 48, 81, 83,
    91, 94, 118, 123, 130
snail 32, 71, 89, 105, 132, **136**
snake 10, 37, 91, 118, 122
sounds 9, 16, 19, 24, 43, 48,
    49, 50, 52, 56, 61, 75, 76,
    80, 86, 95, 102, 104, 105, 107,
    114, 118,137, 141, 146,
    151, 152
sparrow **137**
speed 34, 37, 45, 46, 49, 51, 74,
    80, 81, 83, 100, 113, 115, 123,
    142, 143, 144, 155
spider 32, 42, 92, 125, **138**,
    144
spines 46, 72, 83, 87, 112, 119
squid 7, **98**, 151
squirrel 31, **139**
starfish **140**
sting 22, 40, 46, 78, 119, 125
stork 59
swallow **142**
swan **141**
swift 93, **142**
swordfish **143**

T

tail (prehensile) 12, 33, 82, 84, 95
tarantula **144**
teeth 8, 21, 30, 48, 55, 73, 80, 96,
    101, 112, 117, 127, 130, 136,
    139, 149, 152
tentacles 40, 46, 78, 94, 98
termite 6, **11**, 12, 15, 36, 76
tiger 29, 31, **145**
toad 9, **64**, 144
tongue and taste 6, 12, 33, 61, 65,
    83, 118, 122, 136, 146
tortoise 46, **147**
toucan 146
trout 124
turkey 35
turtle 8, 122, **147**
tusk 55, 73, 149

V

vulture 62, **148**

W

wallaby 79
walrus **149**
wasp **22**, 32, 77, 125
weasel **150**
whale 39, 80, 92, 93, **151**
wildebeest 13, 48, 93
wings 7, 19, 24, 43, 51, 53, 61,
    75, 77, 81, 100, 107, 141,
    142, 148
wolf 25, 38, 47, 56, 120, **152**
wombat **82**
wood louse 32, 46
worm 18, 32, 110, 121, **153**

Y

yak 154

Z

zebra 17, 86, **155**
zooplankton 92

The publisher would like to thank the following for contributing to this book:

Photographs
Page 3, 4 Lyndon Parker; 6 Planet Earth Pictures; 8 Tony Stone Images; 10 Lyndon Parker; 12, 14, 15, 16 Oxford Scientific Films; 17 Lyndon Parker; 18, 19, 23, 24 Andy Teare Photography; 26, 27 Oxford Scientific Films; 29, 30 Lyndon Parker; 34 Oxford Scientific Films; 35 Lyndon Parker *t*, Oxford Scientific Films *b*; 37 Oxford Scientific Films; 38 Lyndon Parker; 39 Lyndon Parker *t*, Oxford Scientific Films *m*; 41 Lyndon Parker; 42 Oxford Scientific Films; 43 Planet Earth Pictures; 45, 47 Lyndon Parker; 48, 50, 51 Oxford Scientific Films; 52 Andy Teare Photography; 53 Oxford Scientific Films; 54 Planet Earth Pictures; 56 Planet Earth Pictures *t*, Oxford Scientific Films *mr*, *ml*; 57, 58 Lyndon Parker; 60 Oxford Scientific Films; 62 Lyndon Parker *t*, *mr*, Oxford Scientific Films *ml*; 63 Andy Teare Photography *t*, Lyndon Parker *b*; 66, 67, 69 Lyndon Parker; 70 Planet Earth Pictures *t*, Oxford Scientific Films *m*; 72 Lyndon Parker *tr*, Andy Teare Photography *tl*; 74 Lyndon Parker; 75 Tony Stone Images *ml*, Oxford Scientific Films *b*; 81, 82 Oxford Scientific Films; 83, 84 Andy Teare Photography; 88, 89 Oxford Scientific Films; 90 Lyndon Parker; 91 Oxford Scientific Films; 92 Lyndon Parker *t*, Eye of Science/Science Photo Library *b*; 94 Oxford Scientific Films; 95 Andy Teare Photography; 97 Planet Earth Pictures; 99 Oxford Scientific Films; 101 Andy Teare Photography *t*, Oxford Scientific Films *br*; 102 Andy Teare Photography; 103 Oxford Scientific Films; 104 Lyndon Parker; 105 Andy Teare Photography; 108 Lyndon Parker; 110, 112, 113 Oxford Scientific Films; 114 Lyndon Parker *ml*, *mr*, Oxford Scientific Films *b*; 115 Lyndon Parker; 116 Planet Earth Pictures; 117 Oxford Scientific Films; 118, 122 Lyndon Parker; 124 Oxford Scientific Films; 125 Andy Teare Photography; 126 Lyndon Parker; 127, 128, 129 Oxford Scientific Films; 131, 132, 133 Lyndon Parker; 134 Andy Teare Photography *t*, Oxford Scientific Films *m*; 135, 137, 138 Oxford Scientific Films; 140 Oxford Scientific Films *t*; Planet Earth Pictures *m*; 141 Andy Teare Photography; 142 Planet Earth Pictures; 144 Oxford Scientific Films *m*, Lyndon Parker *b*; 146 Planet Earth Pictures; 147 Andy Teare Photography; 148 Planet Earth Pictures; 149, 152 Oxford Scientific Films; 153 Lyndon Parker; 154, 155 Oxford Scientific Films

Artists
Graham Allen, Norman Arlott, Mike Atkinson, Craig Austin, Peter Barrett, Caroline Bernard, Robin Bouttell (Wildlife Art Agency), Peter Bull, John Butler, Robin Carter (Wildlife Art Agency), Jim Channel, Dan Cole (Wildlife Art Agency), David Cook, Richard Draper, Brin Edwards, Cecelia Fitzsimons (Wildlife Art Agency), Wayne Ford (Wildlife Art Agency), Chris Forsey, Ray Greenway, Nick Hall, Darren Harvey (Wildlife Art Agency), David Holmes, Steve Howes, Mark Iley (Wildlife Art Agency), Ian Jackson (Wildlife Art Agency), Martin Knowelden, Terence Lambert, Mick Loates, Bernard Long, Andrew Macdonald, Alan Male (Linden Artists, Ltd.), David Marshall, Doreen McGuinness, Brian Mcintyre, G. Melhuish, William Oliver, R.W. Orr, Nicki Palin, Bruce Pearson, Andie Peck (Wildlife Art Agency), Bryan Poole, Clive Pritchard (Wildlife Art Agency), John Rignall (Linden Artists, Ltd.), Steve Roberts (Wildlife Art Agency), Bernard Robinsons, Eric Robson (Garden Studio Illustrators' Agents), G. Robson, Mike L. Rowe (Wildlife Art Agency), Peter David Scott (Wildlife Art Agency), Guy Smith (Mainline Design), M. Stewart (Wildlife Art Agency), Mike Taylor (Garden Studio Illustrators' Agents), Joan Thompson, Treve Tamblin, Guy Troughton, Wendy Webb, Lynne Wells (Wildlife Art Agency), David Whatmore, Ann Winterbottom, David Wood (Wildlife Art Agency), David Wright, T. K. Wayte (David Lewis Management)

Models
Zak Broscombe Walker, Kechet Buckle Zetty, Martha Button, Jennifer Ching, Yazmina Faiz, Ellie French, Jonathan Hodgson, Christopher Jones, Peter Kemp, Ellie Kemp, Daniel MacArthur Seal, Jamie Nazareth, Jack Nazareth, Julia Nazareth, Iynn-ade Odedina, Okikade Odedina, Michael Rego, Rudi Russell, Leila Sowahan